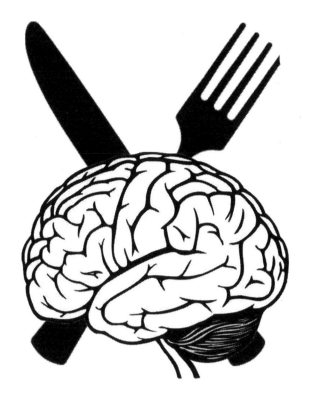

WHO ATE MY MEMORIES?

MEMORY ACTIVITY BOOK

For Adult

This book is specially made for

....

> "
>
> *My dearest friend,*
>
> *You have been working so hard for such a long span. Now, you may have started feeling the effects of ageing, like weakness in your body or signs of dementia. It's completely understandable to feel frustrated when you recently forget someone's name, miss an appointment, or struggle to recall memories from the past. But don't worry, my dear. I know your will is powerful, and you never give up on improving yourself. Yes, you have a strong desire to learn and explore more about this beautiful world, and you can keep doing it. Remember that you are not alone, I follow every step you take and guide you on your upcoming journey.*
>
> *With love,*
>
> "
>
> *Savvy Mind Press*

INSTRUCTION

Fun games in **Who Ate My Memories? Memory Activity Book For Seniors** are exciting and entertaining, and they can also improve memory, daily life skills, and overall mental health.

Let's find out benefits you can gain in this book:

• Help enhance seniors' concentration and focus.

• Help seniors enhance memory skills, including recall, recognition, and retention, leading to better overall memory function.

• Help seniors revise the vocabulary, grammar, communication, and more.

• Help seniors improve addition, subtraction, multiplication, division, and more.

• Stimulate various cognitive abilities, such as planning, time management, and organization, leading to better overall cognitive function in seniors.

INSTRUCTION

- Facilitate social interaction among seniors and promote socialization, bonding, and connection with others.

- Challenge seniors to think critically, analyze information, and make logical decisions.

- Challenge seniors to think logically, plan, and organize steps sequentially.

- Stimulate seniors' visual processing abilities to analyze visual information, patterns, and relationships.

- Help seniors recall past experiences and events and foster a sense of identity.

- Help seniors exercise their memory and concentration skills and improve their cognitive abilities and mental agility.

- Help seniors relax and reduce stress.

HOW TO USE THIS BOOK

Sit upright comfortably. Gently close your eyes. Relax your body. Breathe in and breathe out for at least ten counts before starting.

Read the instructions carefully before solving an activity. You can select the category you wish to improve the most or start the book from the beginning and play the games and puzzles in order.

Activities are divided into three levels, from easy to challenging in each topic. Therefore, you can easily choose the activity that most suits you.

LEVEL OF EACH ACTIVITY:

Easy: ★☆☆

Medium: ★★☆

Challenging: ★★★

TABLE OF CONTENTS

ATTENTION

Connect the dots and answer the question.

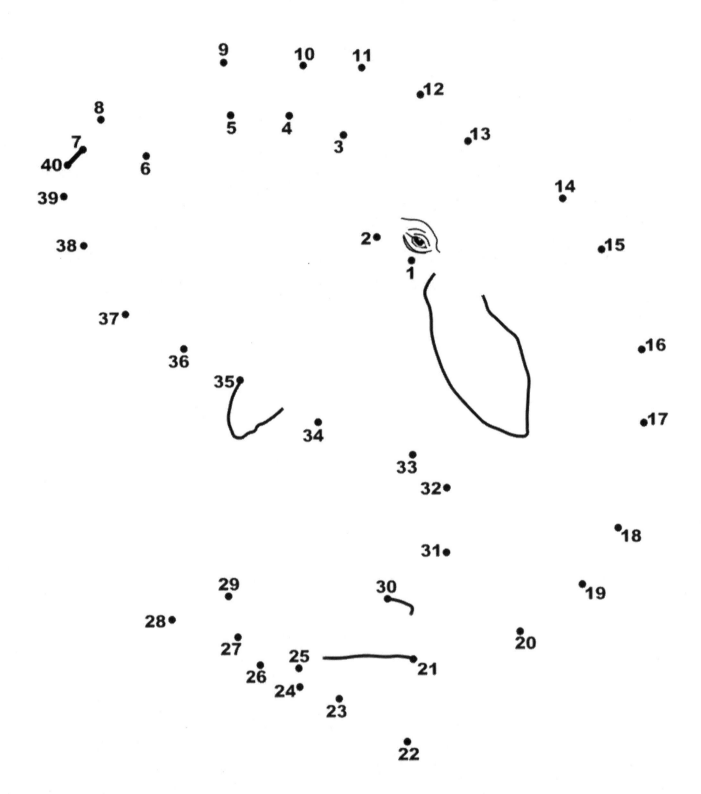

Draw the way to the camping site.

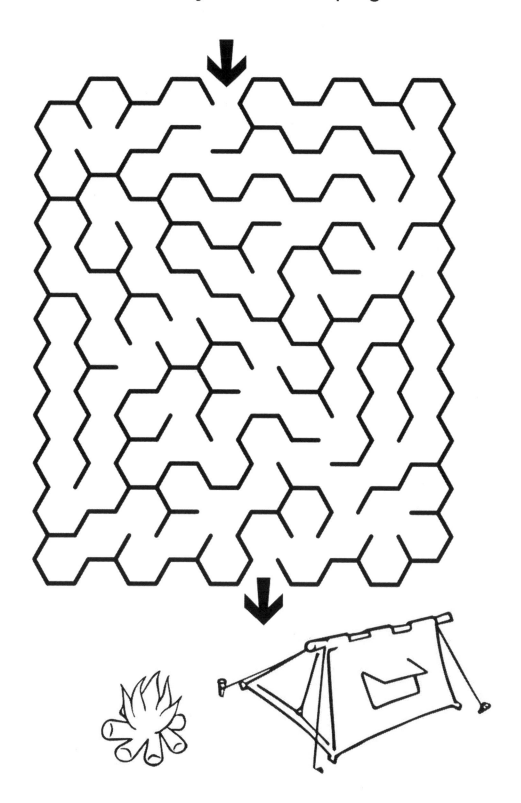

FUN FACT: Camping can relieve stress and depression.

From Smallest To Largest

Arrange the images from smallest to largest.

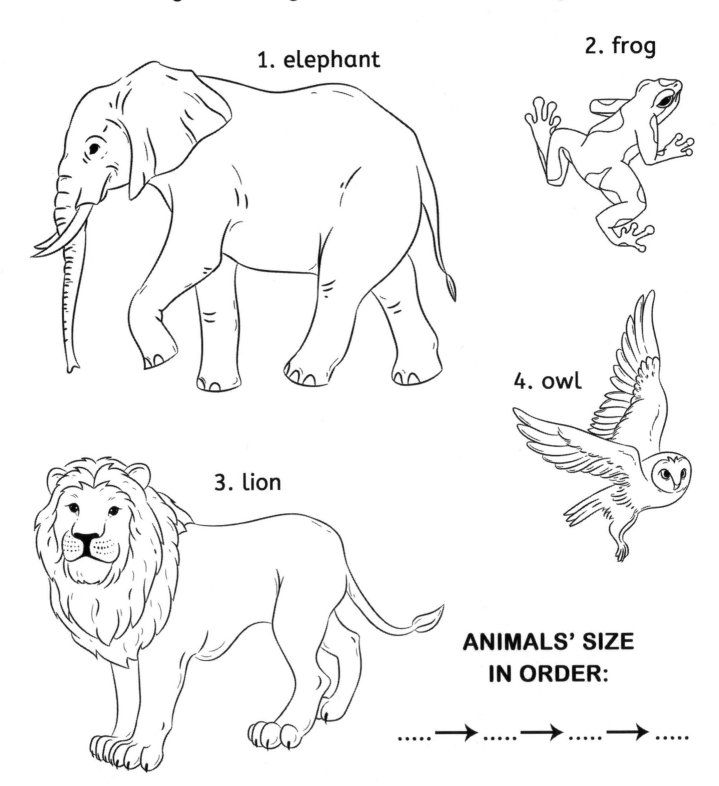

1. elephant

2. frog

4. owl

3. lion

ANIMALS' SIZE IN ORDER:

..... ➞ ..... ➞ ..... ➞ .....

FUN FACT: A lion's roar can be heard five miles away.

Circle the beetle that is different from the others.

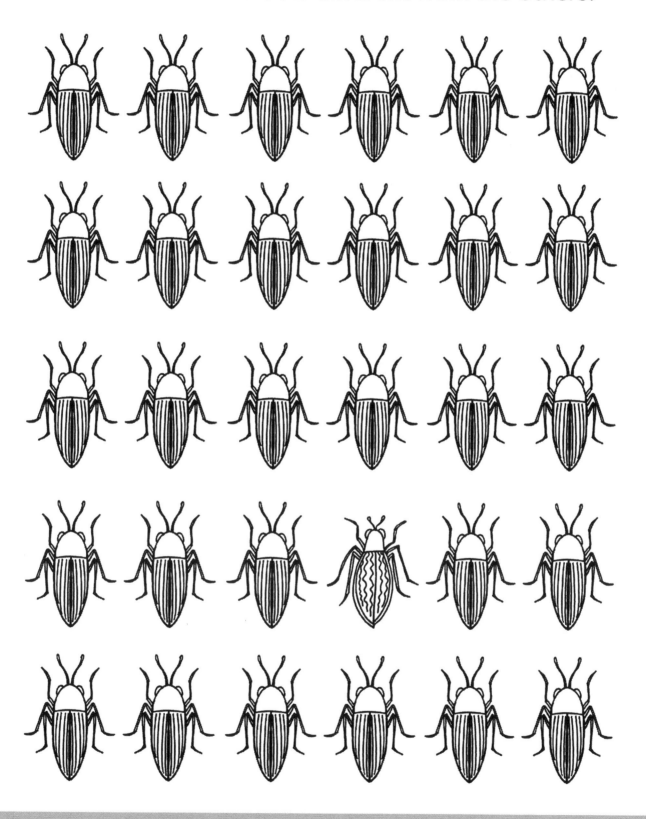

FUN FACT: *Bees have 5 eyes and 6 legs.*

Find and circle the mushroom
hidden in the picture.

FUN FACT: Mushrooms don't need light to grow.

★★☆

Cross out any words that are
repeated more than once.

Camellia	Marigold	Carnation
Gladiolus	Lilac	Rose
Geranium	Poinsettia	Hydrangea
Snapdragon	Dahlia	Peony
Poppy	Rose	Iris
Aster	Daffofil	Daisy
Lavender	Sunflower	Tulip
Magnolia	Lily	Orchid

FUN FACT: Roses are considered as timeless gifts of love.

Circle the pairs of numbers that make 10.

6 9	4 3	2 8
1 4	1 9	1 1
5 5	1 4	8 9
7 3	7 7	4 6
1 2	6 8	2 3
5 8	3 9	0 9

FUN FACT: Every odd number contains the letter E.

 **GARDEN**

★★☆

Circle the picture differently from the others.

Picture 1   Picture 2

Picture 3   Picture 4

FUN FACT: *Plants can hear what is happening around them.*

14

Find and circle 5 differences between two pictures.

FUN FACT: *Village life is calm and peaceful.*

★ ★ ★

Find and circle the different butterfly.

MEMORY

Shake It Off

Close to You

Good for Brain

Good For Health

Complete the Journal

Remember the Images

Remember the Words

Order of Objects

Remember the Names

Remember the Dates

Check the situation(s) that you have encountered.

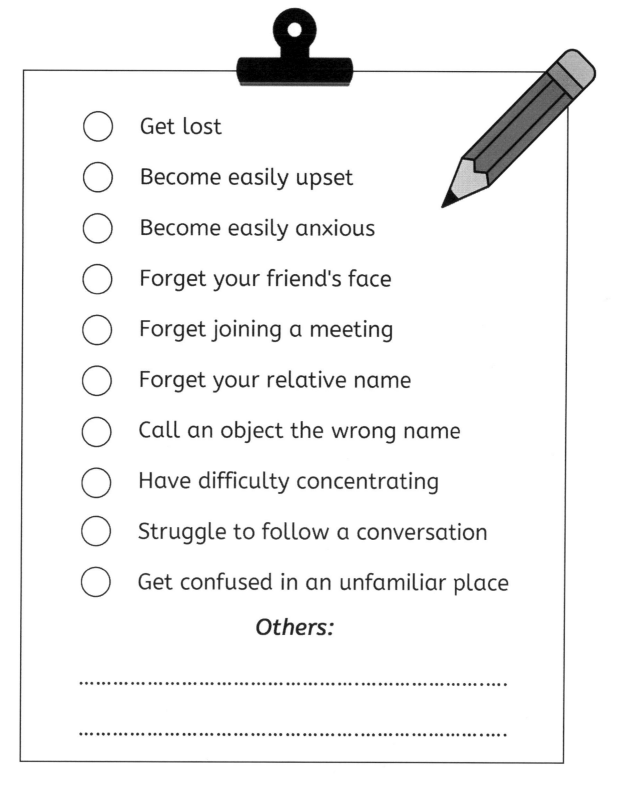

- ◯ Get lost
- ◯ Become easily upset
- ◯ Become easily anxious
- ◯ Forget your friend's face
- ◯ Forget joining a meeting
- ◯ Forget your relative name
- ◯ Call an object the wrong name
- ◯ Have difficulty concentrating
- ◯ Struggle to follow a conversation
- ◯ Get confused in an unfamiliar place

Others:

....

....

FUN FACT: *The ability to forget is a sign of high intelligence.*

Check the item(s) that you often use in a week.

- ◯ Bed
- ◯ Chair
- ◯ Lamp
- ◯ Book
- ◯ Cane
- ◯ Glasses

- ◯ Television
- ◯ Telephone
- ◯ Clock
- ◯ Bag
- ◯ Plate
- ◯ Money

Which object evokes your positive emotion? Why?

....

....

....

....

....

FUN FACT: There are over 129 million books in existence.

Check the food(s) that you eat this week.

○ Blueberries   ○ Tomatoes

○ Salmon   ○ Greek yogurt

○ Walnuts   ○ Black beans

○ Broccoli   ○ Chicken

○ Avocado   ○ Pumpkin

○ Eggs   ○ Red bell peppers

Which foods do you like the most? Why?

....

....

....

....

....

FUN FACT: *Strawberries could cure your headache.*

Check the activities that you do to stay healthy.

○ Meditation   ○ Go to bed early

○ Do yoga   ○ Learn a new skill

○ Cook meals   ○ Eat balanced diet

○ Play puzzles   ○ Join book club

○ Color pictures   ○ Sleep well

○ Go swimming   ○ Do exercises

Which activities do you like the most? Why?

....

....

....

....

....

FUN FACT: The strongest muscle in the body is the tongue.

Fill in the blanks with your daily activities.

⭕ 9:00 AM: ....

⭕ 9:30 AM: ....

⭕ 10:00 AM: ....

⭕ 11:00 AM: ....

⭕ 12:30 PM: ....

⭕ 1:30 PM: ....

⭕ 2:15 PM: ....

⭕ 3:00 PM: ....

⭕ 4:00 PM: ....

⭕ 4:30 PM: ....

⭕ 5:30 PM: ....

⭕ 6:30 PM: ....

⭕ 7:30 PM: ....

FUN FACT: *Humans spend 1/3 of their life sleeping.*

Look at the set of objects for 30 seconds.
Then, use something to cover all the objects.

Write down as many objects as you can remember.

....

....

....

FUN FACT: "Jacket" comes from the French word jaquette.

Look at the box of words for 30 seconds.
Then, use something to cover all the words.

Movies	Celebrity	Sports	Festival
Song	Dance	Awards	Pop culture
Book	Comedy	Fashion	Recreation
Games	Concerts	Event	Animation

1. Could you find the word "event" in the box?

....

2. How many words in the plural form?
Can you write them down?

....

....

....

FUN FACT: The Mona Lisa has no eyebrows.

⭐⭐☆

Look at the set of objects for 1 minute.
Then, use something to cover all the objects.

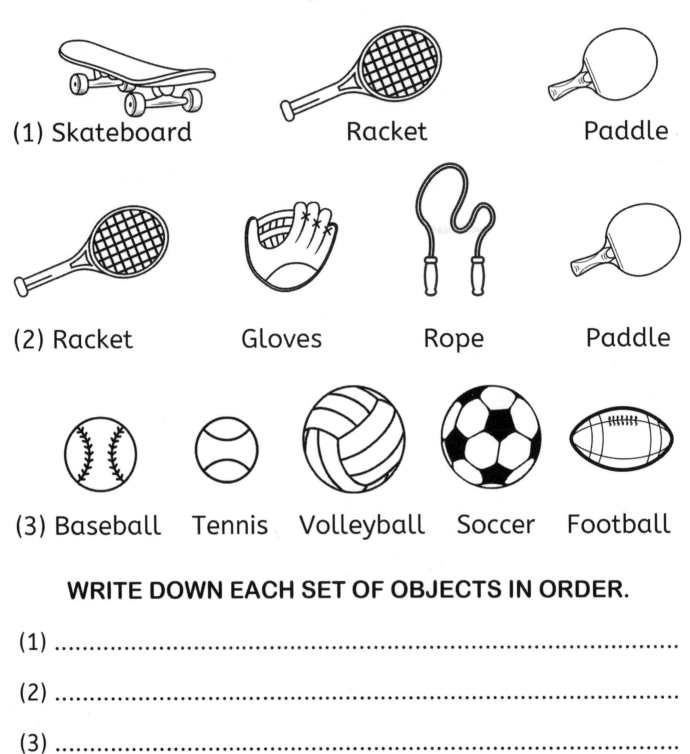

(1) Skateboard   Racket   Paddle

(2) Racket   Gloves   Rope   Paddle

(3) Baseball   Tennis   Volleyball   Soccer   Football

WRITE DOWN EACH SET OF OBJECTS IN ORDER.

(1) ....

(2) ....

(3) ....

FUN FACT: All baseball fields have identical infields.

★ ★ ★

Look at the portraits and names for 2 minutes.
Then, use something to cover all the portraits and names.

Ethan   Naomi   Benjamin   Moira

Write down the name of each portrait.

_____   _____   _____   _____

FUN FACT: *The popular boy name over the past 100 years is James.*

Look at the dates of birth (DOB) for 2 minutes.
Then, use something to cover all the portraits and DOB.

11/02/1962   23/07/1970   07/04/1988   25/12/1955

Write down the correct date of birth for each portrait.

_____   _____   _____   _____

FUN FACT: *Newborn babies can hear as well as you do.*

CHAPTER 3

LANGUAGE

Word Search

Missing Letter

Word Scramble

Crossword

Form a Word

Word Ending

Rhymes

Synonyms & Antonyms

Word Ladder

Rebus

★☆☆

Circle the words that are hidden
diagonally, vertically and forward.

```
H H M L E T T U C E P A Z Q
L A I S G R E E N B E A N S
B A C V P E A S U N K A L E
G R R A I I P L X C R Q N C
A I O T U A N C A J I M H A
E A G C I L S A M J F G X B
M F R E C C I P C G P Q K B
R J E L I O H F A H G L R A
F U E E G T L O L R W J M G
F S N R S X X I K O A I L E
I G S Y P L A X V E W G S B
Y R W Z S M P G V B Q E U U
O B U C C K P M D Q H H R S
D W U W B L V N I O Q T Z F
```

  **WORD LIST**

Artichoke	Cabbage	Green beans	Microgreens
Asparagus	Cauliflower	Kale	Peas
Broccoli	Celery	Lettuce	Spinach

FUN FACT: *Kale is a good source of vitamins A, C and K.*

Fill in the missing letters to complete
the word related to the book genre.

BOOK GENRES

(1) My __ t __ ry

(2) R __ manc __

(3) F __ nta __ y

(4) F __ cti __ n

(5) Th __ ill __ r

(6) C __ m __ dy

(7) P __ __ try

(8) Adv __ ntur __

(9) M __ m __ ir

(10) Bi __ gra __ hy

FUN FACT: *The most sold book is the Bible.*

Unscramble the names of the seafoods

(1)   MRSPHI   _____

(2)   CBAR   _____

(3)   TOSRBEL   _____

(4)   MOLNSA   _____

(5)   NTAU   _____

(6)   MSCLA   _____

(7)   RYSOSET   _____

(8)   LSUSMSE   _____

(9)   UQDSI   _____

(10)   LLOSCSAP   _____

FUN FACT: *Shrimp are excellent swimmers.*

Solve the crossword puzzles to
find the correct countries.

Across

3. Capital city of United Kingdom
7. Capital city of United States
8. Capital city of Germany
9. Capital city of China
10. Capital city of France

Down

1. Capital city of Russia
2. Capital city of Japan
4. Capital city of India
5. Capital city of Brazil
6. Capital city of Egypt

FUN FACT: France is known as L'Hexagone.

Write down as many words as you can make using the letters below.

S	A	T	G	E
N	H	L	D	C
C	O	W	I	D
V	E	L	N	Z

GROUP 1 (3-LETTER WORDS) ....

....

....

GROUP 2 (4-LETTER WORDS) ....

....

....

GROUP 3 (5-LETTER WORDS) ....

....

....

GROUP 4 (6-LETTER WORDS) ....

....

FUN FACT: The longest English word has almost 190,000 letters.

★ ★ ☆

Write down the adjectives.

LIST AS MANY ADJECTIVES ENDING IN -Y AS YOU CAN.

....

....

....

....

LIST AS MANY ADJECTIVES ENDING IN -IVE AS YOU CAN.

....

....

....

....

LIST AS MANY ADJECTIVES ENDING IN -FUL YOU CAN.

....

....

....

....

FUN FACT: The most common letter in English is "e".

★★☆

Write down the nouns.

LIST AS MANY NOUNS THAT RHYME WITH "BRAIN" AS YOU CAN.

....

....

....

....

LIST AS MANY NOUNS THAT RHYME WITH "SWEET" AS YOU CAN.

....

....

....

....

LIST AS MANY NOUNS THAT RHYME WITH "FUN" AS YOU CAN.

....

....

....

....

FUN FACT: A compound noun has two or more words.

Write down the words.

LIST AS MANY SYNONYMS OF "POSITIVE" AS YOU CAN.

....

....

....

....

....

....

....

LIST AS MANY ANTONYMS OF "WEAK" AS YOU CAN.

....

....

....

....

....

....

FUN FACT: Positivity helps you live longer.

Read the clues. Then write down the words.
Start at the bottom and climb to the top.

Replace one letter
- earth is one
of these.

Replace one letter
- you eat off these

Add one letter
- somewhere to be

Remove one letter
- how fast you walk

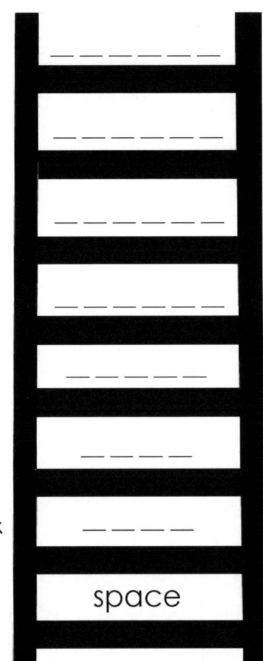

space

Replace one letter
- you fly in them

Add one letter to
make a plural

Replace one letter
- fancy trim for
a dress.

FUN FACT: The first person on the moon was Neil Armstrong.

Guess the words or phrases from the clues
and write them down.

1.

| SECRET ← |
| SECRET |
| SECRET |

_____

2.

Get it
Get it
Get it
Get it

_____

3.

D movie
D movie
D movie

_____

4.

XQQQQQME

_____
_____

5.

Try $\dfrac{stand}{2}$

_____
_____

6.

NO
I

_____
_____

FUN FACT: *Rebus puzzles are incredibly popular in Japan.*

38

CALCULATION

Count the kitchen appliances and write down the correct number for each kind.

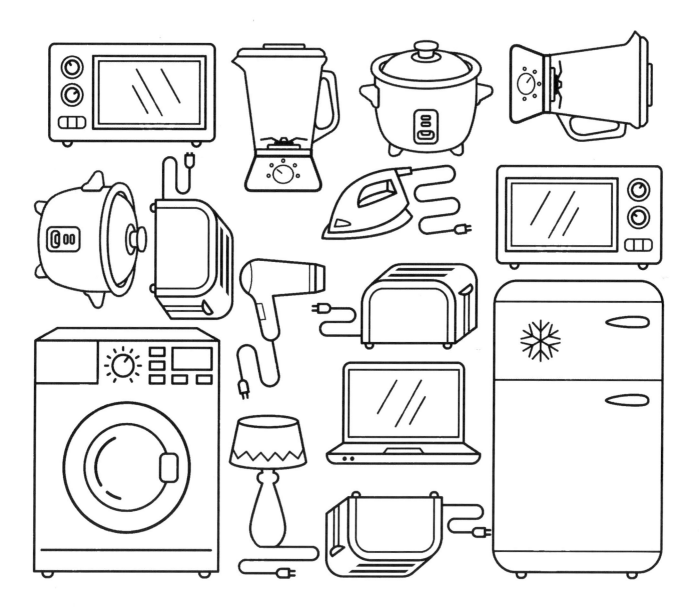

cooker(s): _____   blender(s): _____

refrigerator(s): _____   bread toaster(s): _____

Circle the balls you will put in the holes
to make 30.

★ ☆ ☆

Connect the boxes where the difference is equal to 5.

19 – 14	23 + 22	64 – 32	32 + 13	49 – 4	55 – 10
14 – 9	67 – 22	76 – 31	20 + 25	84 – 84	77 – 32
11 – 6	20 – 15	40 – 35	85 – 45	65-46	68 – 23
32 + 65	86 – 41	18 – 13	57 – 12	99 – 54	35 + 10
98 – 65	69 – 24	20 – 15	15 – 10	8 – 3	46 + 12
24 + 32	33 + 12	45 – 0	39 + 6	22 – 17	100 + 2
37 – 12	45 + 45	17 – 3	78 – 33	30 – 25	89 – 44

FUN FACT: The subtraction of a number from itself gives 0.

Fill in the blanks with the correct numbers.

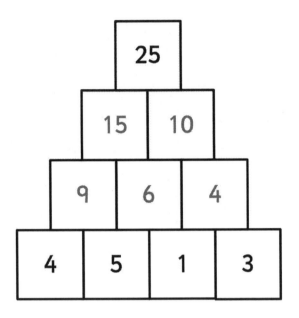

example: 25 = 15+10
15 = 9+6, 10 = 6+4

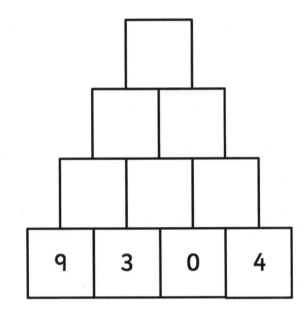

1.

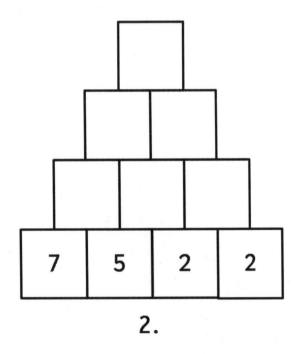

2.

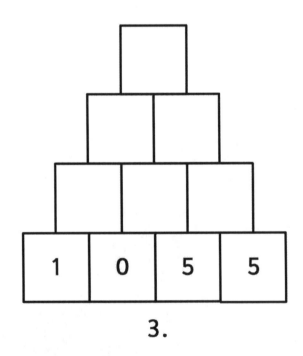

3.

FUN FACT: Adding zero to a number gives the number itself.

★★☆

Fill in the blanks with the correct numbers.

1.

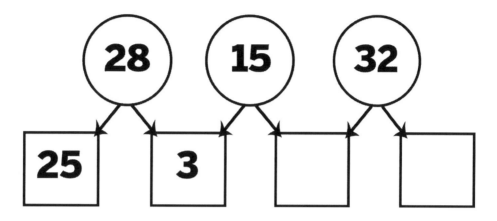

2.

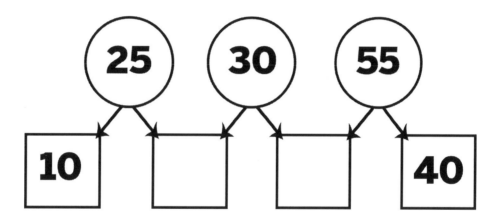

3.

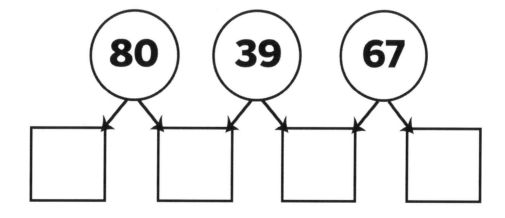

FUN FACT: *2D shapes are shapes with two dimensions.*

★ ★ ☆

Check the price for each food.
Write down the total bill for each order.

Burger	$3
Coffee	$2.5
Hotdog	$1.5
French Fries	$2
Soda	$1.5

MENU

CUSTOMER 1

1 Soda

2 Hotdogs

3 Burgers

TOTAL BILL: $..................

CUSTOMER 1

1 Coffee

1 French Fries

5 Hotdogs

TOTAL BILL: $..................

FUN FACT: *French fries' origin was found in Belgium.*

Fill in the blanks with the correct numbers.

1.

7	×	27	=	189
×		÷		×
45	÷	9	=	
=		=		=
	×	3	=	945

2.

15	÷	3	=	5
×		×		×
	÷	10	=	
=		=		=
600	÷	30	=	20

3.

58	×		=	870
×		÷		÷
3	×		=	15
=		=		=
174	÷	3	=	58

4.

58	÷	29	=	
×		×		×
15	÷	5	=	
=		=		=
870	÷	145	=	6

FUN FACT: *The product of any number multiplied by a 'zero' is zero.*

Fill in the blanks with the correct numbers.

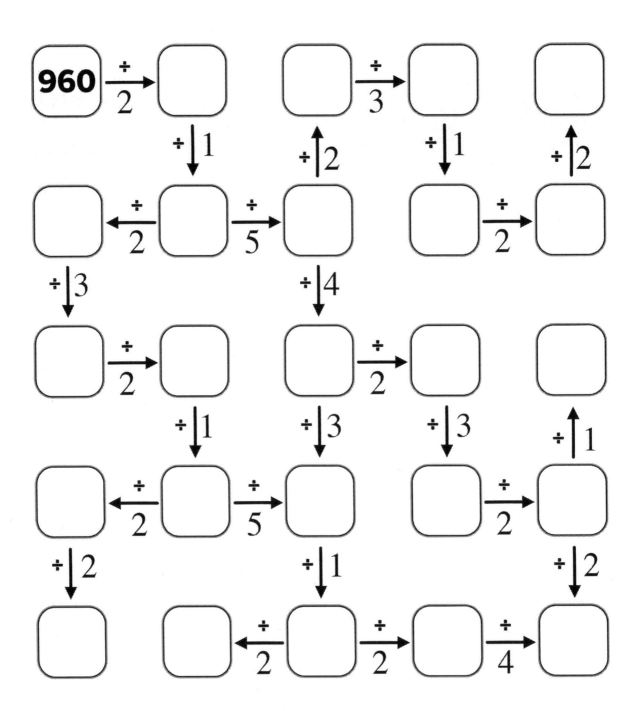

FUN FACT: *Odd numbers are not divisible by 2.*

47

⭐⭐⭐

Solve the task and write down the correct number.

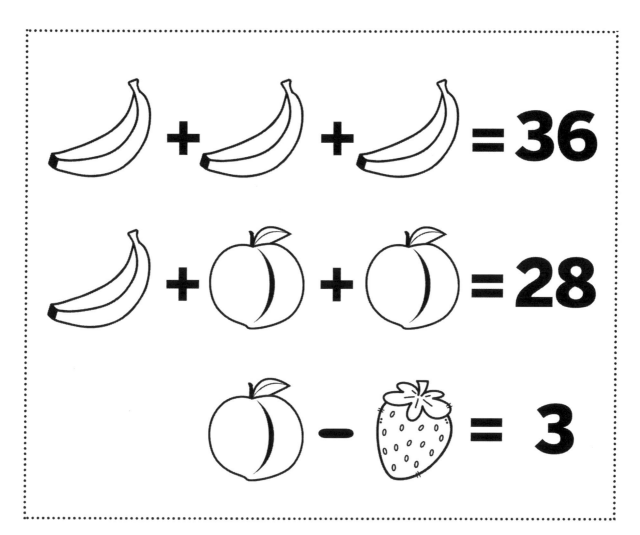

THERE ARE

....

FUN FACT: Apples are members of the rose family.

Solve the task and write down the correct number.

IF

5 + 9 = 16

4 + 6 = 4

3 + 8 = 25

Then

1 + 2 = ?

THE ANSWER IS

....

FUN FACT: There is no Roman numeral for zero.

CHAPTER 5

EXECUTIVE FUNCTIONING

Checklist

Find & Count

Correct the Spelling

Explore the World

Task Initiation

Organization

Planning

Management

Self-control

Discussion

Check to evaluate executive functioning skills.

- ○ Do you remember to submit work on time?

- ○ Do you execute sets of tasks in series as planned?

- ○ Do you have control over his feelings before acting out?

- ○ Do you show structure and organization in your work?

- ○ Do you prioritize what has to be done first?

- ○ Do you give thoughts before making a decision or taking action on you?

- ○ Do you remember all the knowledge and facts on the required subjects?

- ○ Can you read well, clearly, and without making mistakes in pronunciation and sounds?

- ○ Can you write clearly, accurately, quickly, and with the ability to convey your message?

FUN FACT: *Humans are not the only species that can dance.*

Answer the question below.

HOW MANY HENS WITH 3 LEGS ARE THERE?

There are .... hens with 3 legs.

FUN FACT: Most farms in the U.S. are family farms.

Below are words that have been misspelled.
Write the correct spelling of each word in the blank.

1. suprise

_____

2. comming

_____

3. agin

_____

4. tommorrow

_____

5. Febuary

_____

6. wich

_____

7. desided

_____

8. peice

_____

9. wonce

_____

10. shoud

_____

11. becase

_____

12. fourty

_____

13. beutiful

_____

14. thru

_____

FUN FACT: *There are over 1,110 ways to spell sounds in English.*

Check the activities you wish to do in the future.

Sports

- ◯ Miniature golf
- ◯ Bird-watching
- ◯ Tennis
- ◯ Kite flying
- ◯ Horse Riding

Crafts

- ◯ Ceramics
- ◯ Woodcraft
- ◯ Quiltmaking
- ◯ Jewelry making
- ◯ Papercraft

Gatherings

- ◯ Miniature golf
- ◯ Bird-watching
- ◯ Tennis
- ◯ Kite flying
- ◯ Horse riding

Outings

- ◯ Theme parks
- ◯ Carnivals
- ◯ County fairs
- ◯ Comedy clubs
- ◯ Concerts

FUN FACT: Your cells change when you learn stuff.

Below are the steps to prepare before cooking.
Arrange these according to your choice of orders.

1 Make a detailed shopping list

2 Ask for help with shopping

3 Find recipes in cookbooks

4 Visualize how the dish will be

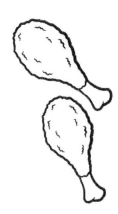

5 Choose your meals

6 Make a prep list

7 Make time to cook

Steps in the order: ....

There are **6** principles of meal planning including adequacy,
balance, calorie (energy) control, nutrient density, moderation
and variety. Underline the one you think is the most important.

FUN FACT: *Fried chicken was invented by the Scottish.*

Circle things you put on the
Thanksgiving dinner table.

Write down what you plan for
a beach trip next week.

TRAVEL PLAN

Budget: _____

Location: _____

Time/Season: _____

_____

Accommodation: _____

Foods & Drinks: _____

_____

Packing: _____

_____

_____

Activities: _____

_____

_____

FUN FACT: *Sand comes in lots of different colors.*

Set time to solve these math puzzles
and write down the answer for each box.

1

35 – 20 – 3 – 7 – 1 = _____

You expect to finish this in _____ minutes.

Start at: _____   End at: _____

Have you finished on time: ◯ Yes   ◯ No

2

23 + 5 – (15 + 14 – 4) = _____

You expect to finish this in _____ minutes.

Start at: _____   End at: _____

Have you finished on time: ◯ Yes   ◯ No

3

(42 ÷ 6 + 9) × 5 – 2 = _____

You expect to finish this in _____ minutes.

Start at: _____   End at: _____

Have you finished on time: ◯ Yes   ◯ No

FUN FACT: France has more than 10 time zones.

Write down what you will manage
to do in these scenarios.

Someone takes your favorite book from you.

You see an open bag of money on a coach.

Someone has just called you a mean name.

FUN FACT: Soft skills are personality traits and behaviors.

Answer the question below.
Share your opinions more.

Why is it important to be happy with yourself?

_____

_____

_____

_____

_____

_____

_____

_____

_____

INSPIRING QUOTE: Life is beautiful and so are you.

CHAPTER 6

INTERACTION

Ask Yourself

Find Something

Mr. Brain Says

Knock Knock

Crack You Up

I Would Rather

Time for Yourself

Crazy Lib

Truth Dare

Story of My Life

51 **SELF-REFLECTION** ★☆☆ **Ask Yourself**

Ask and answer the questions about yourself.

Am I using my time wisely?

◯ YES   ◯ NO

Am I employing a healthy perspective?

◯ YES   ◯ NO

Am I living true to myself?

◯ YES   ◯ NO

Am I taking care of myself physically?

◯ YES   ◯ NO

What am I really scared of?

◯ YES   ◯ NO

What matters most in my life?

◯ YES   ◯ NO

Have I made someone smile today?

◯ YES   ◯ NO

What have I given up on?

◯ YES   ◯ NO

FUN FACT: Self-reflection is the key to self-awareness.

Look around your house and find something ...

☐ .... starts with the first letter of your name.

☐ .... is longer than a pencil.

☐ .... is shorter than a toothbrush.

☐ .... is heavier than your shoe.

☐ .... has the letter B on it.

☐ .... has numbers on it.

☐ .... has four sides.

☐ .... smells good.

☐ .... is green.

☐ .... is smooth.

☐ .... is blue.

☐ .... is red.

☐ .... is round.

☐ .... is smaller than you.

FUN FACT: *Kitchen sinks contain more germs than toilets.*

Follow Mr. Brain's lead and be active.

Mr. Brain says: tap your head.

Mr. Brain says: blink your eyes.

Mr. Brain says: tickle your toes.

Mr. Brain says: rub your tummy.

Mr. Brain says: clap your hands.

Mr. Brain says: count your fingers.

Mr. Brain says: make a cup of tea.

Mr. Brain says: point to your ears.

Mr. Brain says: feel your heartbeat.

Mr. Brain says: draw a star in the air.

Mr. Brain says: make up a silly word.

Mr. Brain says: sing your favorite song.

Mr. Brain says: touch your left shoulder.

Mr. Brain says: smile at someone near you.

Mr. Brain says: stretch as high up as you can.

Mr. Brain says: close your eyes and make a wish.

FUN FACT: *Working out sharpens your memory.*

Join the activity with your family or friends.
You guys take turns asking & answering each Knock Knock joke.

Knock knock.

Who's there?

Weekend.

Weekend who?

Weekend do anything

we want!

Knock knock.

Who's there?

Iva.

Iva who?

Iva sore hand from

knocking so long!

Knock knock.

Who's there?

Adore.

Adore who?

Adore is between us.

Open up!

Knock knock.

Who's there?

Cash.

Cash who?

No thanks, but I'd love

some peanuts!

FUN FACT: *Laughter allows us to manage pain better.*

⭐☆☆

Join the activity with your family or friends.
You guys take turns asking and answering each joke.

1. What did one ocean say to the other ocean?

Nothing, it just waved.

2. How does NASA organize a party?

They planet.

3. Why are crabs so bad at sharing?

Because they're all shellfish.

4. Why didn't the skeleton go to the dance?

Because he had no body to go with.

5. What do you call a belt with a watch on it?

A waist of time.

6. Why did the tomato turn red?

It saw the salad dressing.

FUN FACT: A dad joke is almost always pithy and corny.

★ ☆ ☆

Join the activity with your family or friends.
You guys take turns asking and explaining each question.

1 I would rather cuddle with a fluffy teddy bear
than go to work.

2 I would rather gaze at cute animal videos
than do chores.

3 I would rather wear cute pajamas
than have a cozy movie night.

4 I would rather watch a heartwarming movie
than a serious drama.

5 I would rather have a fluffy pet to play with
than a fancy piece of jewelry.

6 I would rather spend time with adorable kittens
than attend a meeting.

FUN FACT: A teddy bear is the official national symbol of Japan.

Write down your answers for the questions below.

USING 10 WORDS, DESCRIBE YOURSELF.

....

....

MAKE A LIST OF 30 THINGS THAT MAKE YOU SMILE.

....

....

....

....

MAKE A LIST OF EVERYTHING YOU'D LIKE TO SAY "NO" TO.

....

....

MAKE A LIST OF EVERYTHING YOU'D LIKE TO SAY "YES" TO.

....

....

....

FUN FACT: Self-care helps you perform at your best.

Join the activity with your family or friends.
You guys take turns completing the blanks and reading aloud.

MIDDLE SCHOOL MEMORY

One time way back in _____ -grade _____
                      NUMBER   A SUBJECT

class, I _____ badly. At first, I thought it would be
        PAST VERB

_____ or covered by the _____ of other
PAST VERB   CLOTHING ITEM

students chatting. Big surprise it was not. The only person

talking was the _____, who was interrupted by
                   A JOB

_____ cannon-fire farts. She said she was
ADJECTIVE

_____ that I couldn't hold it in and proceeded to tell
PAST VERB

a story of she taught an athlete named _____ who
                                         YOUR NAME

did nearly the same thing. At that time, I just wanted to dig a

hole for myself.

FUN FACT: *Sweet potatoes can cause gas.*

Join the activity with your family or friends.
You guys take turns answering a question or doing an action.

Truth questions

1. What's your biggest fear?

2. What's your biggest fantasy?

3. When was the last time you lied?

4. When was the last time you cried?

5. What's the worst thing you've ever done?

Dare questions

1. Take a weird selfie.

2. Tell the saddest story you know.

3. Howl like a wolf for two minutes.

4. Dance without music for two minutes.

5. Let someone else tickle you, and try not to laugh.

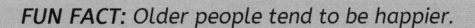

FUN FACT: *Older people tend to be happier.*

Write a story to tell your family or friends
about one of your most fantastic experiences in the past.

CHAPTER 7

REASONING

61 HEALTHY DIET

What Do You Eat?

Circle the green food items.

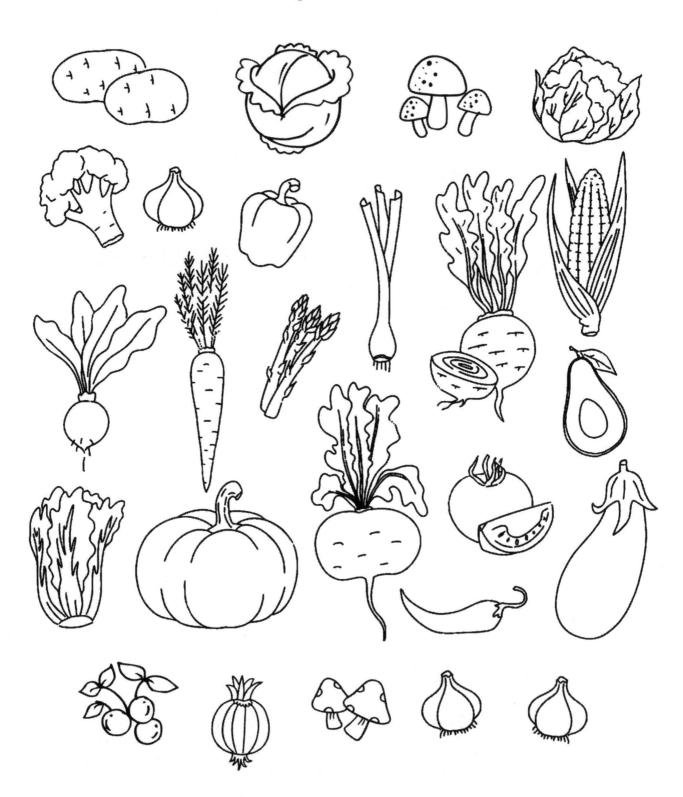

FUN FACT: Kiwi fruit is native to China

73

Circle the animals that live on the ground.

Circle what you wear in the cold winter.

FUN FACT: 'Jingle Bells' was the first song played in space.

Match the place with the correct information.

A.   Libraries   ....

B.   Museums   ....

C.   Schools   ....

D.   Hospitals   ....

E.   Train   ....

F.   Airports   ....

1.   provide medical care and emergency services

2.   provide access to books, information, and more

3.   provide formal education and training

4.   offer educational and cultural experiences

5.   offer access to air travel

6.   provide transportation options

FUN FACT: *The Louvre in Paris has over 35,000 artworks.*

Solids, Liquids & Gas

Categorize the name of these pictures
in the correct column.

SOLIDS

_____

_____

GAS

_____

_____

_____

LIQUID

_____

_____

_____

FUN FACT: Windmills have been in use since 2000 B.C.

66 COUPLE

Match two items are used together.

Circle the item that does not belong to the group.

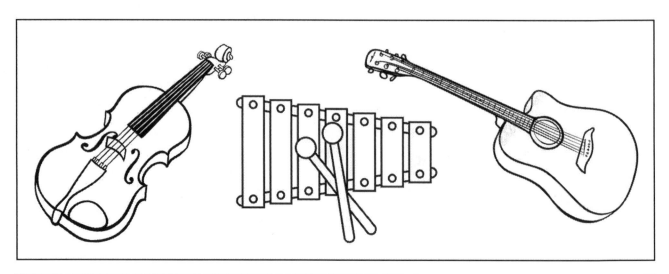

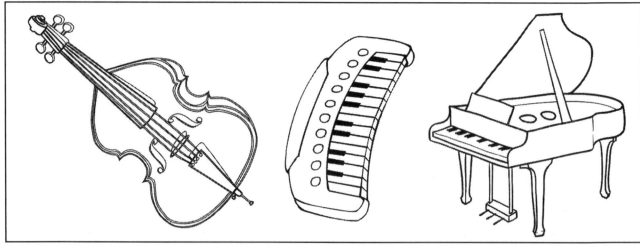

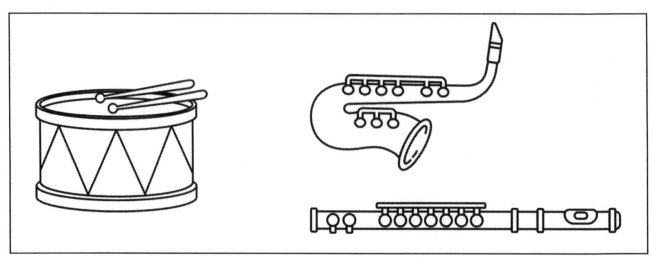

FUN FACT: *The cello dates from the 1500s.*

Fill in the puzzle so that every row across,
every column down and every 2 by 2 box
contains the numbers 1 to 4.

1.

			3
			2
3			
4			

2.

			3
4			
			1
3			

3.

			2
	3		
4			
		2	

4.

			1
	1	3	
4			2

FUN FACT: *Sudoku went viral in the Western world in 2004.*

Play with Numbers 2

Fill in the puzzle so that every row across, every column down and every 3 by 2 by box contains the numbers 1 to 6.

		4	6		
5		3	1		
			4		6
		6			3
4		5	2		
		2			

FUN FACT: *Sudoku does not require any "external knowledge."*

Fill in the puzzle so that every row across,
every column down and every 3 by 3 box
contains the numbers 1 to 9.

9	5				1			2
6	3					1		
		8		6				7
						5		
	6	1	7		9			
		2		4				8
	9							5
	1			5	6	4	8	
	8			1	7			6

FUN FACT: *"Godfather of Sudoku" was Maki Kaji, a Japanese.*

CHAPTER 8

SEQUENCING

How to Draw

Home Workout

Crafting

Write a Journal

How To Cook Pasta

Cycle 1

Cycle 2

If Then

Arrange the Information

Make a Plan

★ ☆ ☆

Follow the step-by-step instructions to draw a T-Rex.

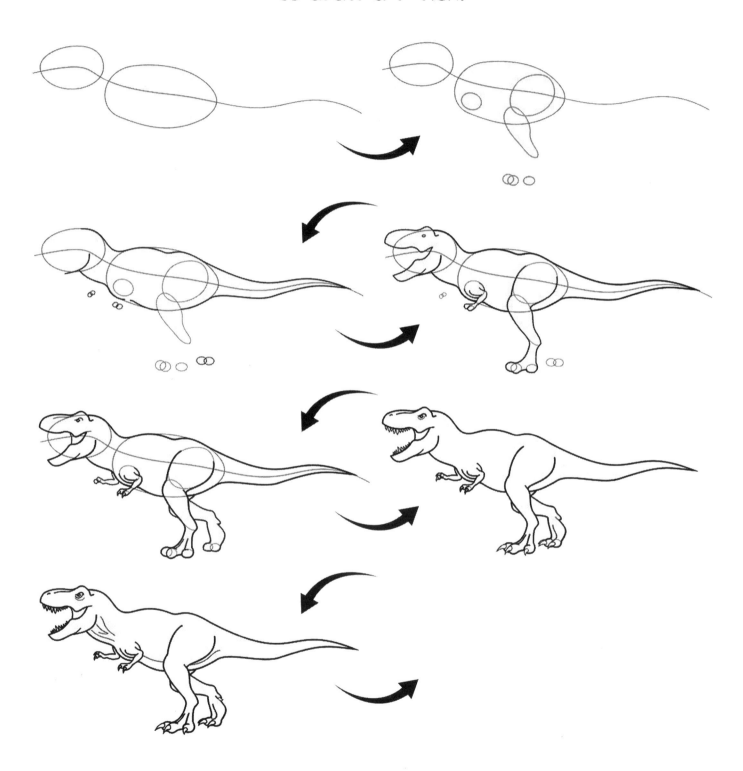

FUN FACT: Dinosaurs were around millions of years ago!

Follow the instructions to relax your body.

1. Warmup

2. Shoulder rolls (flexibility)

3. March on spot (mobility)

4. Ankle (strength)

5. Knee bend (strength)

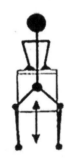

6. Sit to Stand (strength)

7. Calf (stretch)

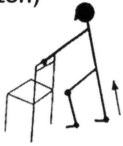

8. Calf (stretch)

FUN FACT: There are about 600 muscles in the human body.

Follow the instructions to make a butterfly.

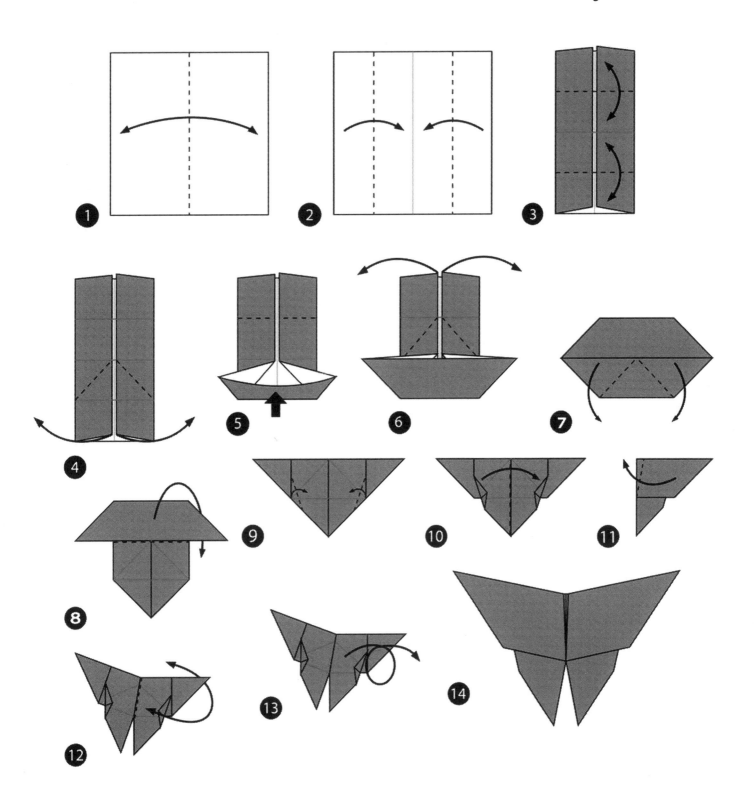

FUN FACT: Origami came to Japan thanks to Buddhist monks.

Write down what you often do in a day in order.

_____

_____

_____

_____

_____

_____

_____

_____

_____

_____

_____

_____

_____

FUN FACT: _Waking up earlier balance your mental health._

Arrange the steps in the correct order.

LET'S COOK PASTA!

STEPS IN THE CORRECT ORDER

..... → ..... → ..... → ..... → ..... → .....

FUN FACT: *Spaghetti is the most popular noodle in america.*

Arrange the pictures in the correct order.

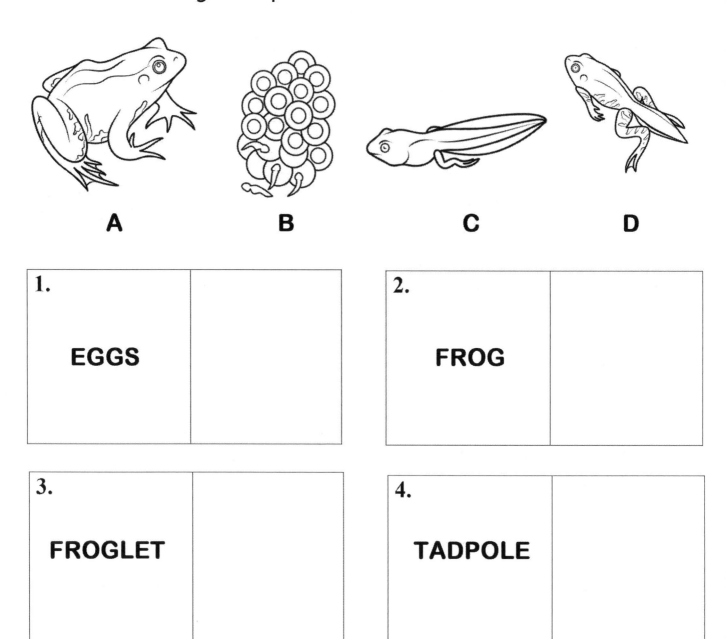

A   **B**   **C**   **D**

1.	
EGGS	

2.	
FROG	

3.	
FROGLET	

4.	
TADPOLE	

STEPS IN THE CORRECT ORDER

..... ➝ ..... ➝ ..... ➝ .....

FUN FACT: *Frogs were the first land animals with vocal cords.*

Check TRUE or FALSE for each statement.

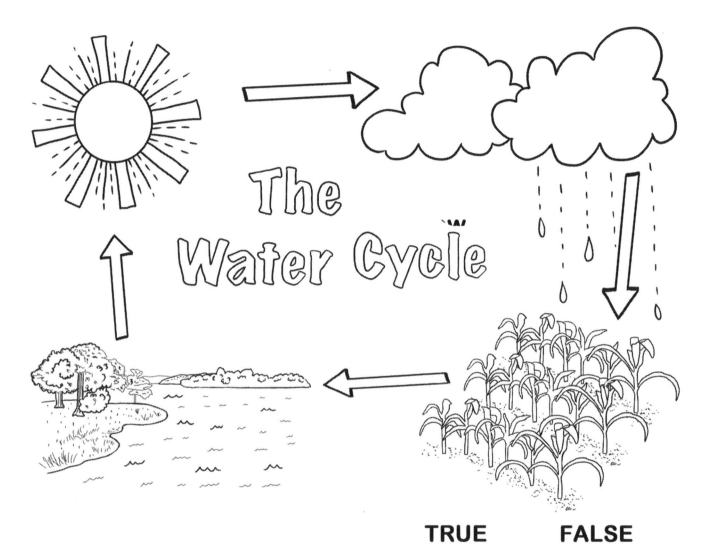

	TRUE	FALSE
1. Rain and snow are precipitation.	☐	☐
2. Evaporation moves up to the sky.	☐	☐
3. There are three main stages in the water cycle.	☐	☐

FUN FACT: *Our bodies are mostly water.*

Join the activity with your family or friends.
You guys take turns to complete the sentence and read aloud.

IF

1. If I were a doctor, I would

2. If I were an engineer, I would

3. If I were a lawyer, I would

4. If I were an architect, I would

5. If I were a pharmacist, I would

6. If I were a chef, I would

7. If I were a scientist, I would

8. If I were an artist, I would

9. If I were a writer, I would

10. If I were an actor, I would

THEN

a. shake my head crazily.

b. stick out my tongue.

c. make silly noises.

d. giggle uncontrollably.

e. hiccup loudly.

f. pick my nose.

g. prank my poor friend.

h. sneeze dramatically.

i. sing a silly song.

j. swim on the floor.

FUN FACT: *The average doctor has about 40,000 hours of training.*

91

Rearrange the sentences to form a story.

(a) His small space was filled with cherished memories, including photos of his late wife and children.

(b) He found joy in the simple things and took pleasure in each day.

(c) At 68, Mr. Lee lived in a small apartment in the city.

(d) He spent his days reading books, listening to music, and leisurely walks through the park.

(e) His kind smile and warm spirit made him a beloved figure in the community.

THE STORY IN THE CORRECT ORDER

..... → ..... → ..... → ..... → .....

INSPIRING QUOTE: Let go of the past and not wait for the future.

92

★ ★ ★

Write a detailed plan for a family meeting.

FUN FACT: *We can find creative ideas when we meet new people.*

VISUAL-SPATIAL SKILL

Circle the shadow of the picture.

★☆☆

Check the card appears the same
when it was turned upside down.

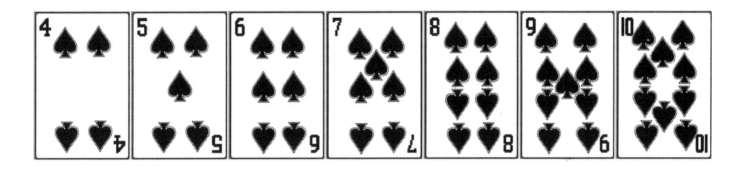

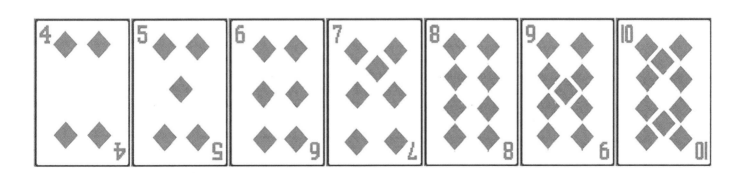

FUN FACT: *Poker is 100% a game of skill in the long run.*

★★☆

Follow the direction to find the place
and circle the correct answer.

Where is the GARDEN?

Take the first left after the main entrance, follow the path
past the bridge, then you'll see it in front of you at the end.

A   B   C   D   E   F   G   H

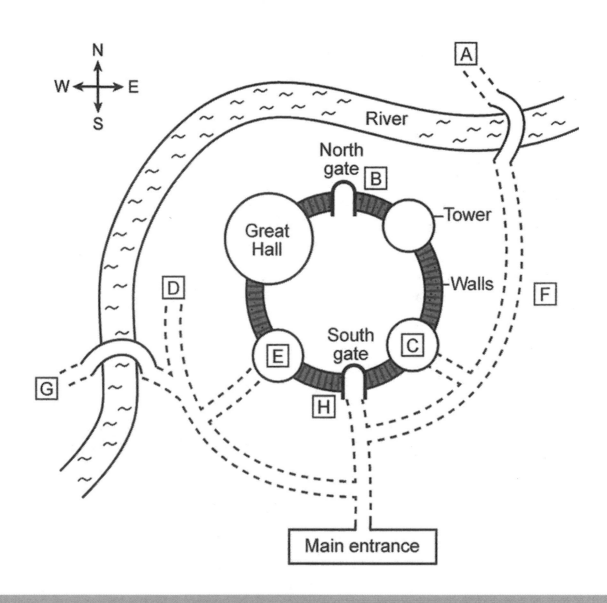

FUN FACT: Castles were built for protection.

Complete the world map using the clues above.

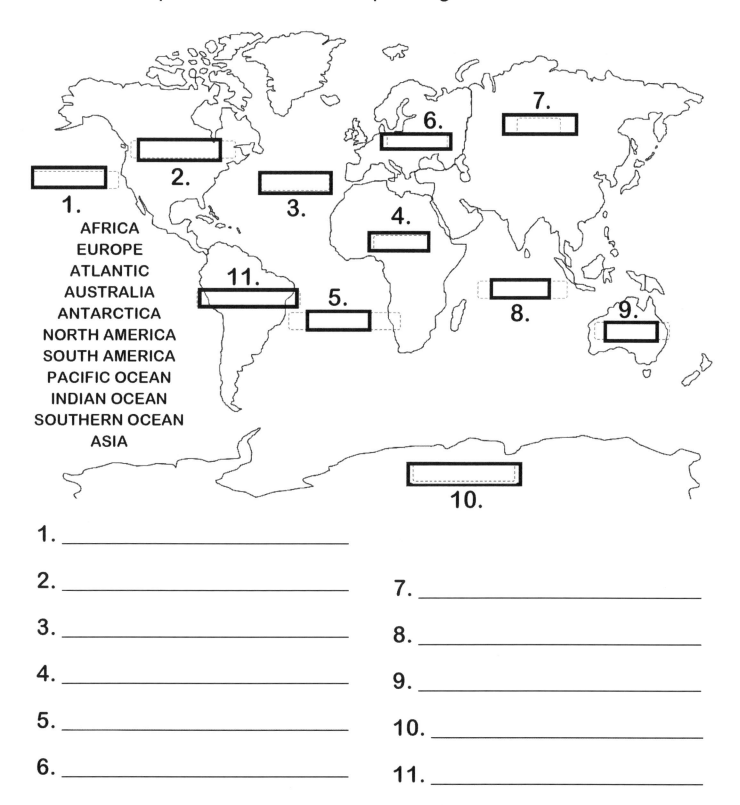

AFRICA
EUROPE
ATLANTIC
AUSTRALIA
ANTARCTICA
NORTH AMERICA
SOUTH AMERICA
PACIFIC OCEAN
INDIAN OCEAN
SOUTHERN OCEAN
ASIA

1. _____

2. _____

3. _____

4. _____

5. _____

6. _____

7. _____

8. _____

9. _____

10. _____

11. _____

FUN FACT: *Earth is the third closest planet to The Sun.*

Circle the biggest state of the U.S.

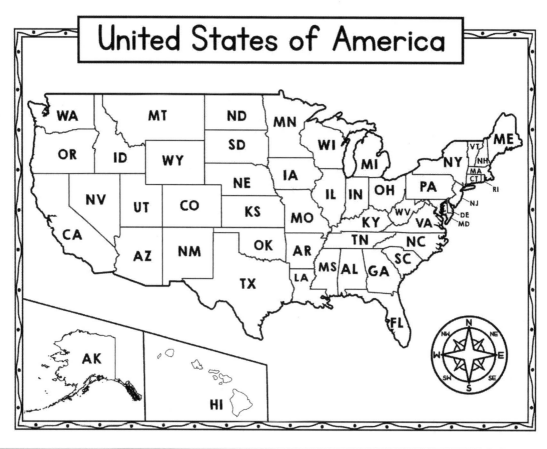
United States of America

Alabama	Hawaii	Massachusetts	New Mexico	South Dakota
Alaska	Illinois	Michigan	New York	Tennessee
Arizona	Idaho	Minnesota	North Carolina	Texas
Arkansas	Indiana	Mississippi	North Dakota	Utah
California	Iowa	Missouri	Ohio	Vermont
Colorado	Kansas	Montana	Oklahoma	Virginia
Connecticut	Kentucky	Nebraska	Oregon	Washington
Delaware	Louisiana	Nevada	Pennsylvania	West Virginia
Florida	Maine	New Hampshire	Rhode Island	Wisconsin
Georgia	Maryland	New Jersey	South Carolina	Wyoming

FUN FACT: The United States has no official language.

★★☆

Circle the correct reflected shapes.

1.

A   B   C   D

2.

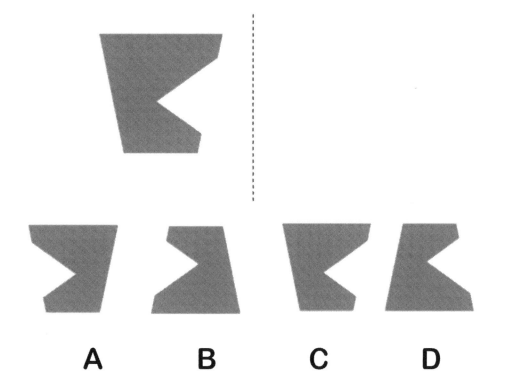

A   B   C   D

FUN FACT: Mirrors can cause hallucinations.

Match the following.

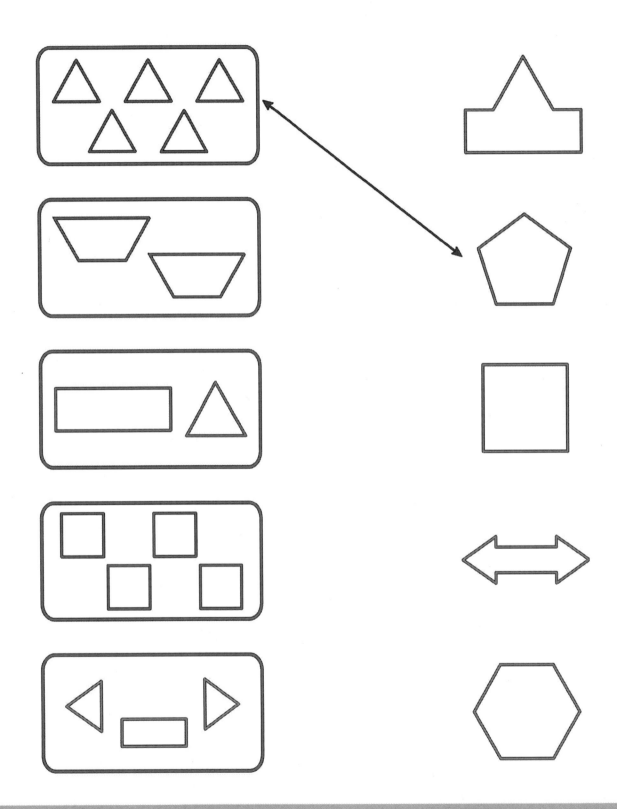

Find and write down the number of each object.

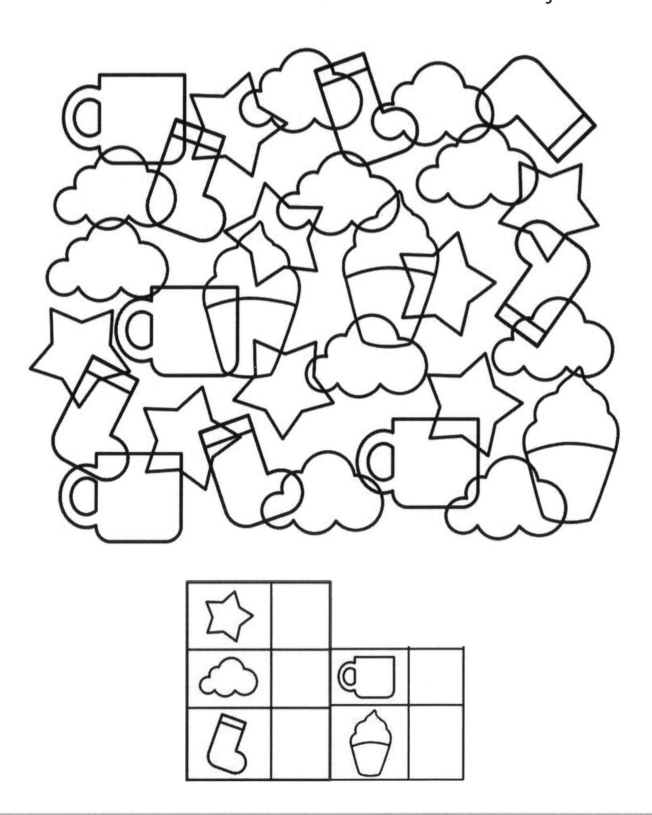

★★☆

Circle the number that is shown by base-10 blocks.

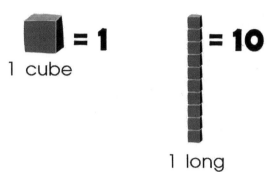 = 1
1 cube

= 10
1 long

= 100
1 flat

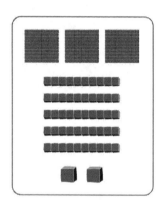

132   312

352   230

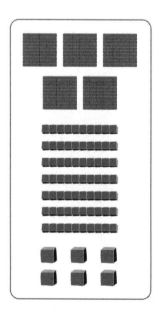

756   675

575   576

★★★

Circle the 3D shape that can be made
from the 2D net.

1. Which 3D shape can be made from the 2D net?

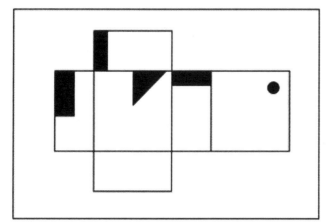

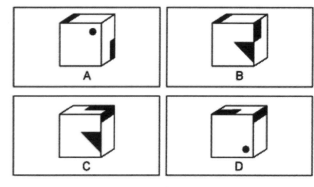

The answer is ....

2. Which figure is a rotation of the object?

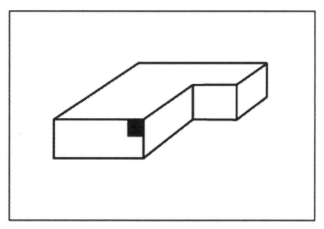

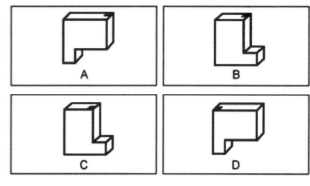

The answer is ....

FUN FACT: *In everyday life, we inhabit a space of three dimensions.*

REMINISCENCE ACTIVITIES

Trivia Questions

Complete the Text

Crossword

Word Search

Spot the Difference

True/ False Questions

Complete the Years

Match the Information

Arrange the Events

Answer the Questions

Circle the correct answer.

1. Who was the British King during the war?

A. George II

B. Edward VIII

C. George III

D. William IV

2. Which American general turned traitor and joined the British?

A. Benedict Arnold

B. Marquis de Lafayette

C. George Washington

D. Daniel Morgan

3. America received foreign aid from what country?

A. Portugal

B. Switzerland

C. Sweden

D. France

4. Who wrote the Declaration of Independence?

A. Thomas Jefferson

B. Andrew Jackson

C. George Washington

D. John Hancock

5. Where was the last major battle of the war ?

A. Yorktown

B. Saratoga

C. Long Island

D. Ticonderoga

FUN FACT: Some British soldiers were actors by night.

Copy the correct words to fill in the blanks.

The Civil War was a major conflict fought between 1861 and

(1) _____, primarily over the issue of slavery and

states' rights. The war was fought between the Union, comprised

of the northern states, and the Confederacy, comprised of the

southern states, which seceded from the (2) _____.

The war resulted in the deaths of an estimated 620,000 (3)

_____, making it one of the deadliest in American

history.   The   Union   emerged   victorious,   and   (4)

_____ was abolished due to the war. However, the

war's aftermath also led to a long (5) _____ period

and racial tension in the United States.

slavery   soldiers   1865   Union   reconstruction

FUN FACT: More than 3 million men fought in the war.

Solve the crossword puzzles.

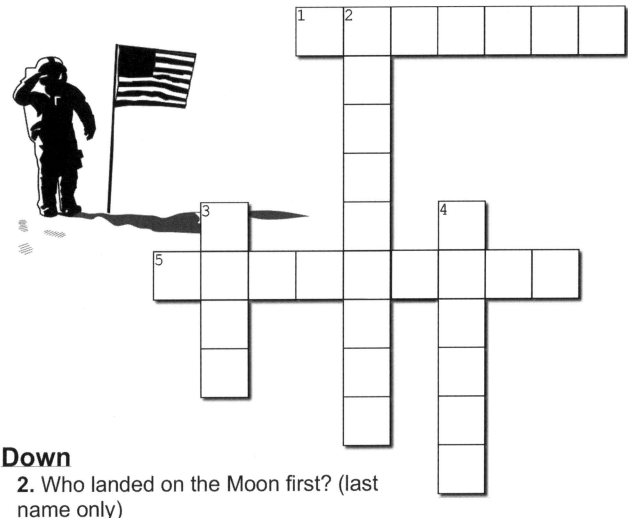

Down

2. Who landed on the Moon first? (last name only)

3. In which month did the astronauts return to Earth?

4. Which Apollo landed on the moon first?

Across

1. 'That's one small step for man, one giant leap for _____.'

5. Which was erected on the Moon during the Apollo program?

FUN FACT: *Neil Armstrong had musical talents.*

Circle the words hidden diagonally,
vertically and forward.

```
H C H I L D R E N X H E F Y S S
C O M F O R T A O Y S R Q N R C
T Y A E L U G C K A M Y A A W O
E C V R Z Q L Z E K T R C T E N
L J Z T U S W R A I E W G G O S
E A K I V F C I R T E C Y I S U
V A H L S N X E E N K M T D P M
I R C I I H P V M Q O A R Y A E
S V I T Y S D Q S N L A P Q P R
I E X Y O Z H E O U C L Q J A I
O G R R K J D C P T T A E S R S
N R P N I I E O I Y I T U Q T M
S D R P J K P D M A Q Z J X M C
D C O U N T E R C U L T U R E C
M R L P V R S U B U R B S K N C
E K A J C P O S T W A R X O T U
```

WORD LIST

Apartment	Counterculture	Increase	Prosperity
Children	Creditcards	Newcars	Suburbs
Comfort	Economy	Population	Televisions
Consumerism	Fertility	Postwar	Veterans

FUN FACT: Baby boomers are living longer than previous generations

Find and circle 7 differences
between two pictures.

List some rock songs that you like:

_____

_____

_____

FUN FACT: *The electric guitar remains the symbol of rock music*

Check TRUE or FALSE for each statement.

DRIVE-IN
date night

	TRUE	FALSE

1. The first drive-in theater opened in 1953. ☐ ☐

2. In the 1950s, drive-in theaters were popular destinations for teenagers on dates. ☐ ☐

3. Some drive-ins had "car hops" who would bring food and drinks to patrons' cars. ☐ ☐

4. The 1970s saw a decline in drive-in theaters due to the rise of 3D theater. ☐ ☐

5. Some drive-ins had large screens, with some measuring up to 200 feet wide. ☐ ☐

6. Some drive-ins had "buck nights," where patrons could get into the movies for just $1. ☐ ☐

7. Some drive-ins offered special screenings for charity or non-profit organizations. ☐ ☐

FUN FACT: The first patented drive-in was opened in New Jersey.

Fill in the blank with the
correct year for each history event.

1. _____: Theodore Roosevelt became President.

2. _____: The United States entered World War I.

3. _____: The stock market crashed, marking the beginning of the Great Depression.

4. _____: The Japanese attacked Pearl Harbor to enter World War II.

5. _____: President John F. Kennedy was assassinated.

6. _____: The Civil Rights Act was passed.

7. _____: Neil Armstrong became the first person to walk on the moon.

8. _____: President Richard Nixon resigned from office following the Watergate scandal.

FUN FACT: Roosevelt was a prolific writer.

★★★

Match the phrase in column A with
the one in column B to complete the information.

A

(1). The US's first women's rights convention _____

(2). The National Organization for Women (NOW) _____

(3). The Equal Pay Act of 1963 prohibits _____

(4). The term "glass ceiling" was coined to _____

(5). The Violence Against Women delivered _____

(6). The first female Supreme Court justice was _____

(7). The National Women's Political Caucus was _____

(8). The first Women's Strike for Equality _____

B

(a). federal resources to combat domestic violence.

(b). founded to encourage women's political participation.

(c). marked the 50th anniversary of women's suffrage.

(d). appointed in 1981.

(e). was founded in 1966.

(f). wage discrimination based on gender.

(g). was held in New York in 1848.

(h). describe the invisible barrier to women's advancement in the workplace.

FUN FACT: *Feminism refer to equal rights for women*

★★★

Arrange the events in the correct order.

(1). CDC used the term "AIDS" for the first time.

(2). President Bush signed the Ryan White HIV/AIDS Treatment Extension Act.

(3). The AIDS information booklet was sent to every household in America.

(4). First antiretroviral drug, AZT, approved by the FDA for treatment of AIDS.

(5). Princess Diana shook hands with an AIDS patient.

(6). The first known cases of AIDS were reported in Los Angeles and New York City.

(7). UNAIDS set the goal of ending the AIDS epidemic by 2030.

..... $\longrightarrow$ ..... $\longrightarrow$ ..... $\longrightarrow$ ..... $\longrightarrow$ ..... $\longrightarrow$ ..... $\longrightarrow$ .....

FUN FACT: There are no vaccines to prevent or treat HIV.

Read the passage and
write the answer for each question.

The 1900s saw the development and use of nuclear weapons in wars. In 1945, the first atomic bombs were dropped on Hiroshima and Nagasaki by the US, ending World War II. This event marked a turning point in world history as the destructive power of nuclear weapons became apparent. During the Cold War, the US and the Soviet Union engaged in a nuclear arms race, with the two countries developing and testing increasingly powerful weapons. The threat of nuclear war loomed worldwide for decades, with many fearing a catastrophic global conflict. However, the end of the Cold War in 1991 saw a significant reduction in nuclear weapons stockpiles and a renewed focus on disarmament and nonproliferation efforts.

1. What two cities did the US bomb in Japan?

_____

2. Besides the US, who had nuclear weapons in the Cold War in the text?

_____

FUN FACT: Nuclear energy releases zero carbon emissions.

LOGIC PUZZLES & BRAIN TEASERS

Count the Ducks

Find the Missing

Riddles

Spot the Number

Crack the Code

Matchstick Puzzles

How many?

IQ Games

Logic Puzzle 1

Logic Puzzle 2

★ ☆ ☆

Count the ducks and write down the answer.

HOW MANY DUCKS ARE THERE?

_____

Circle the missing dice to complete the set.

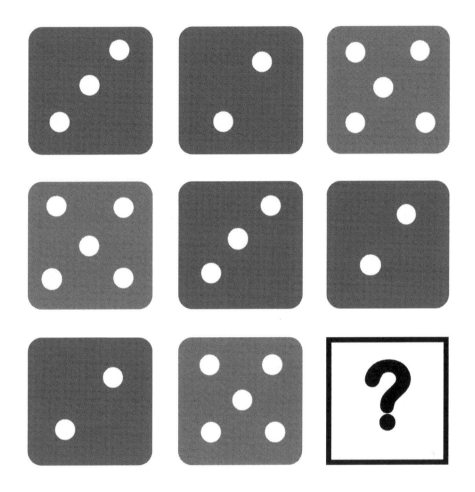

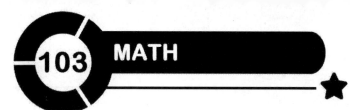

★★☆

Read and answer the riddles.

1. A family has five sons, each of them has a sister. How many kids does a family have in total?

The answer: _____

2. Two math books complain to each other. What do they tell each other?

The answer: _____

3. Isabella has a huge family: 20 cousins, ten aunts, and ten uncles. Each cousin has an aunt who's not Isabella's. How is that possible?

The answer: _____

4. Mom baked 24 cookies for six kids. How many cookies does each of them get?

The answer: _____

5. Which month has 28 days in it?

The answer: _____

6. It's midnight now, and it's raining. The weather forecast says it will be warm and sunny for the next two days. Will it be sunny in 48 hours?

The answer: _____

FUN FACT: Zero is an even number.

Write down the correct car's parking spot number.

THE CAR'S PARKING SPOT NUMBER:

_____

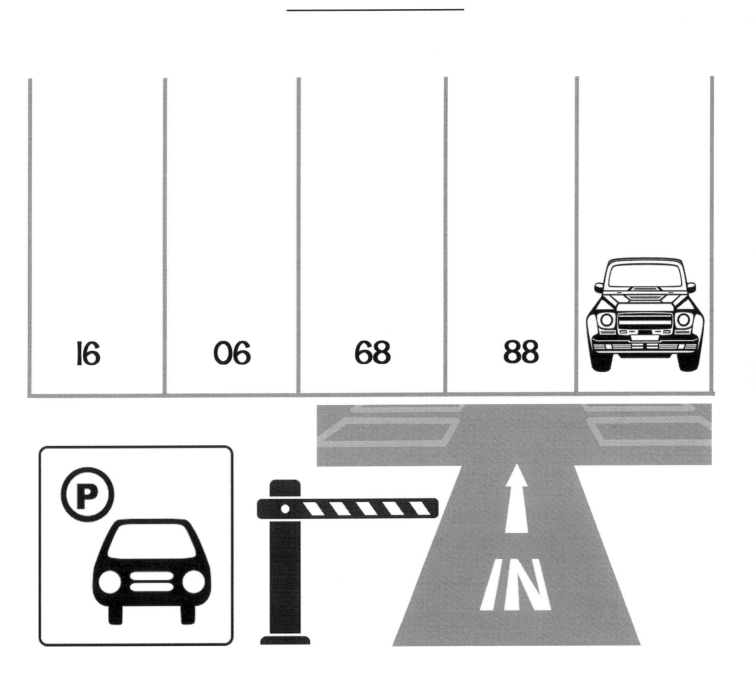

16   06   68   88

FUN FACT: Most car horns are in the key of F.

★★☆

Use the clues to crack the code.

| 6 | 8 | 2 | one number is correct and well placed |

| 7 | 3 | 8 | nothing is correct |

| ? | ? | ? | 2 | 0 | 6 | two numbers are correct but wrong places |

| 6 | 1 | 4 | one number is correct but wrong placed |

| 7 | 8 | 0 | one number is correct but wrong placed |

THE CORRECT ANSWER IS

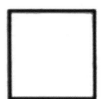  

FUN FACT: Over 50% use their name or birthdate in their password.

Read the clues and rearrange the matchsticks
to solve the puzzles.

**Move 3 matchsticks to get
5 squares**

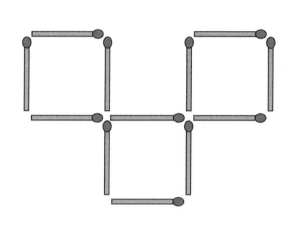

**Remove 6 matchsticks
leaving no triangles**

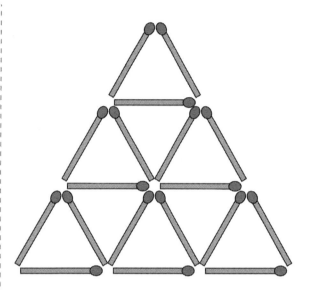

**Add 5 matchsticks to
get a 9**

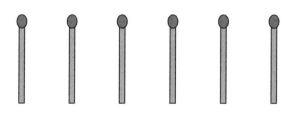

**Move 2 matchsticks to get
3 triangles**

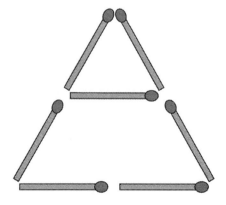

FUN FACT: A flame's color is affected by the oxygen supply.

★★★

Find out how many shapes and write
the number in the blank.

1. There are _____ squares.

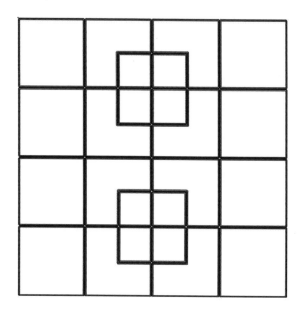

2. There are _____ squares.

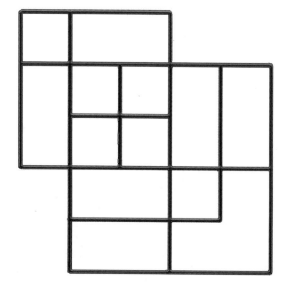

FUN FACT: *A perfect sphere does appear in nature.*

INTELLIGENCE

Answer the Questions.

Circle the correct answer.

1. Which is the missing section?

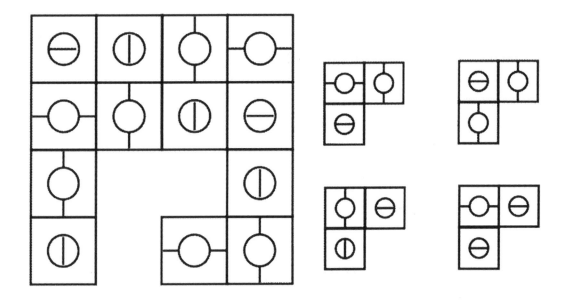

2. Which pentagon should come next?

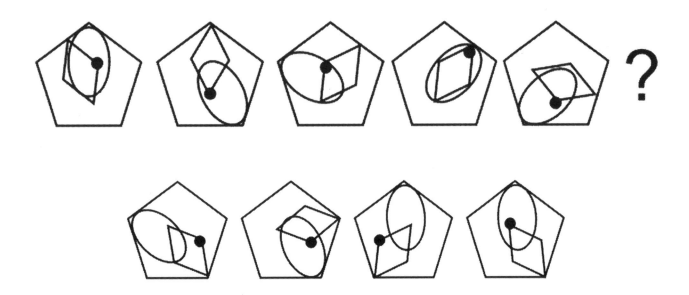

FUN FACT: *Intelligent people ask good questions.*

Solve the logic puzzle and check the correct answer.

Ann is an aspiring author and writes blogs. She writes 10 hours a day for 3 straight consecutive days and then rests on the following day. During one particular week, she wrote on Thursday, Friday, and Saturday. Did she write on her blog the Wednesday of this same week?

YES ☐

NO ☐

FUN FACT: In 2021, the average blog post length was 1416 words.

Solve the logic puzzle and write down the answer.

A girl meets a lion and unicorn in the forest. The lion lies every Monday, Tuesday and Wednesday and the other days he speaks the truth. The unicorn lies on Thursdays, Fridays and Saturdays, and the other days of the week he speaks the truth. "Yesterday I was lying," the lion told the girl. "So was I," said the unicorn. What day is it?

THE ANSWER IS _____ .

COLORING ACTIVITIES

Mandala

Inspiring Quote

Landscape

Flowers

02 CAMPING

03 WILD ANIMALS

ANIMALS' SIZE IN ORDER:

.2. → .4. → .3. → .1.

04 INSECTS

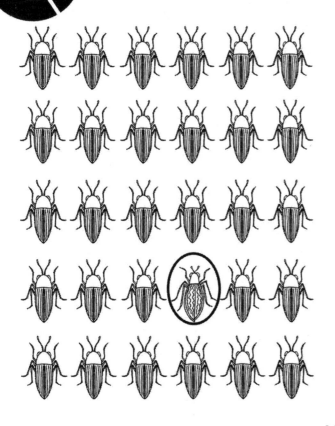

05 MUSHROOM

137

06 FLOWERS

Camellia	Marigold	Carnation
Gladiolus	Lilac	~~Rose~~
Geranium	Poinsettia	Hydrangea
Snapdragon	Dahlia	Peony
Poppy	~~Rose~~	Iris
Aster	Daffofil	Daisy
Lavender	Sunflower	Tulip
Magnolia	Lily	Orchid

07 NUMBERS

6 9	4 3	(2 8)
1 4	(1 9)	1 1
(5 5)	1 4	8 9
(7 3)	7 7	(4 6)
1 2	6 8	2 3
5 8	3 9	0 9

08 GARDEN

Picture 1

Picture 2

(Picture 3)

Picture 4

09 COUNTRYSIDE

10 BUTTERFLIES

16 FASHION

The answers are not necessary in order:

trousers/pants,

jacket/cap/coat, dress,

shoes, scarf, T-shirt, hat

17 ENTERTAINMENT

1. No.

2. 5 words in the plural form:

Movies, Games, Concerts,

Sports, Awards

18 SPORTS

(1) Skateboard Racket

Paddle

(2) Racket Gloves Rope

Paddle

(3) Baseball Volleyball

Tennis Soccer Football

19 NAMES

Naomi   Moira   Ethan   Benjamin

20 DATE OF BIRTH

23/07/1970   25/12/1955   11/02/1962   07/04/1988

21 VEGETABLES

```
H H M L E T T U C E P A Z Q
L A I S G R E E N B E A N S
B A C V P E A S U N K A L E
G R R A I I P L X C R Q N C
A I O T U A N C A J I M H A
E A G C I L S A M J F G X B
M F R E C C I P C G P Q K B
R J E L I O H F A H G L R A
F U E E G T L O L R W J M G
F S N R S X X I K O A I L E
I G S Y P L A X V E W G S B
Y R W Z S M P G V B Q E U U
O B U C C K P M D Q H H R S
D W U W B L V N I O Q T Z F
```

22 BOOKS

(1)   Mystery

(2)   Romance

(3)   Fantasy

(4)   Fiction

(5)   Thriller

(6)   Comedy

(7)   Poetry

(8)   Adventure

(9)   Memoir

(10) Biography

23 SEAFOODS

(1) SHRIMP
(2) CRAB
(3) LOBSTER
(4) SALMON
(5) TUNA
(6) CLAMS
(7) OYSTERS
(8) MUSSELS
(9) SQUID
(10) SCALLOPS

24 TRAVELING

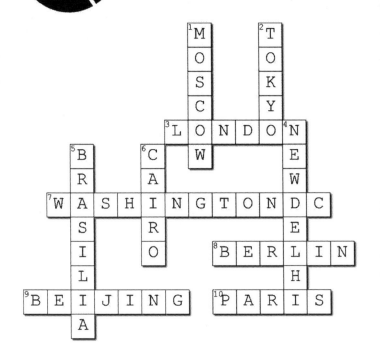

25 WORDS

GROUP 1 (3-LETTER WORDS)
win, lid, own, owl, owe, old, now, low, how, hat, has, did, cow, ash, eco, sat, ice, leo

GROUP 2 (4-LETTER WORDS)
love, wild, show, shoe, salt, noel, nice, lice, lash, echo, chat, aloe, cons, cold, snow, wide, what, than, dice, wind, halt, halo, glow, hole, hold

GROUP 3 (5-LETTER WORDS)
width, whole, shown, shove, salon, novel, lance, glide, glove, vowel

GROUP 4 (6-LETTER WORDS
shovel, glance, decile

26 ADJECTIVES

ADJECTIVES ENDING IN -Y:
happy, funny, comfy, shiny, rainy, cheery, tasty, fluffy, cozy, windy, witty, steady, fruity, sticky

ADJECTIVES ENDING IN -IVE:
positive, creative, active, sensitive, productive, progressive, supportive, constructive, adaptive, assertive, stimulative, incentive, amative, magnetic

ADJECTIVES ENDING IN -FUL:
beautiful, wonderful, joyful, playful, grateful, powerful, delightful, cheerful, peaceful, thoughtful, skillful, successful

27 NOUNS

NOUNS THAT RHYME WITH "BRAIN":
terrain, main, remain, explain, gain, obtain, contain, plane, train, chain, rain, Spain, reign, lane.

NOUNS THAT RHYME WITH "SWEET":
complete, feet, street, meet, heat, eat, concrete, seat, sheet, treat, meat, repeat, wheat, elite.

NOUNS THAT RHYME WITH "FUN":
one, done, son, run, sun, won, gun, ton, nun, bun, stun, lunch, month, chunk.

28 POSITIVE VIBE

SYNONYMS OF "POSITIVE":
optimistic, affirmative, uplifting, inspiring, cheerful, happy, joyful, pleasant, enthusiastic, dynamic, energetic, radiant, vibrant, delighted.

ANTONYMS OF "WEAK":
strong, powerful, mighty, resilient, vigorous, tough, healthy, active, steady, forceful, stable, potent, firm.

29 SPACE TRAVEL

WORDS IN ORDER

planet

planes

plates

places

place

lace

pace

space

30 RANDOM

1. top secret
2. forget it
3. 3D movie
4. excuse me
5. try to understand
6. no idea

31 APPLIANCES

cooker(s): 2

blender(s): 2

refrigerator(s): 1

bread toaster(s): 3

32 BILLIARDS

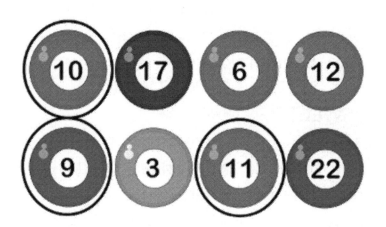

33 SUBTRACTION

19 - 14	23 + 22	64 - 32	32 + 13	49 - 4	55 - 10
14 - 9	67 - 22	76 - 31	20 + 25	84 - 84	77 - 32
11 - 6	20 - 15	40 - 35	85 - 45	65-46	68 - 23
32 + 65	86 - 41	18 - 13	57 - 12	99 - 54	35 + 10
98 - 65	69 - 24	20 - 15	15 - 10	8 - 3	46 + 12
24 + 32	33 + 12	45 - 0	39 + 6	22 - 17	100 + 2
37 - 12	45 + 45	17 - 3	78 - 33	30 - 25	89 - 44

34 ADDITION

```
        22
      15    7
    12    3    4
  9    3    0    4
         1.
```

```
        30
      19    11
    12    7    4
  7    5    2    2
         2.
```

```
        21
      6    15
    1    5    10
  1    0    5    5
         3.
```

35 SHAPES

36 FAST FOOD

1.

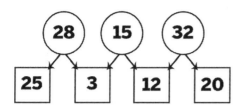

| 28 | 15 | 32 |
| 25 | 3 | 12 | 20 |

2.

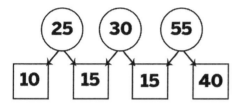

| 25 | 30 | 55 |
| 10 | 15 | 15 | 40 |

3.

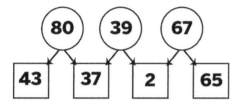

| 80 | 39 | 67 |
| 43 | 37 | 2 | 65 |

CUSTOMER 1
- 1 Soda
- 2 Hotdogs
- 3 Burgers

TOTAL BILL: $13.5

CUSTOMER 1
- 1 Coffee
- 1 French Fries
- 5 Hotdogs

TOTAL BILL: $12

$13.5   **$12**

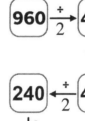

37 MULTIPLICATION

38 DIVISION

1.

7	×	27	=	189
×		÷		×
45	÷	9	=	5
=		=		=
315	×	3	=	945

2.

15	÷	3	=	5
×		×		×
40	÷	10	=	4
=		=		=
600	÷	30	=	20

3.

58	×	15	=	870
×		÷		÷
3	×	5	=	15
=		=		=
174	÷	3	=	58

4.

58	÷	29	=	2
×		×		×
15	÷	5	=	3
=		=		=
870	÷	145	=	6

960 $\xrightarrow{÷2}$ 480   48 $\xrightarrow{÷3}$ 16   4

$÷1\downarrow$ $÷2\uparrow$ $÷1\downarrow$ $÷2\uparrow$

240 $\xleftarrow{÷2}$ 480 $\xrightarrow{÷5}$ 96   16 $\xrightarrow{÷2}$ 8

$÷3\downarrow$ $÷4\downarrow$

80 $\xrightarrow{÷2}$ 40   24 $\xrightarrow{÷2}$ 12   2

$÷1\downarrow$ $÷3\downarrow$ $÷3\downarrow$ $÷1\uparrow$

20 $\xleftarrow{÷2}$ 40 $\xrightarrow{÷5}$ 8   4 $\xrightarrow{÷2}$ 2

$÷2\downarrow$ $÷1\downarrow$ $÷2\downarrow$

10   4 $\xleftarrow{÷2}$ 8 $\xrightarrow{÷2}$ 4 $\xrightarrow{÷4}$ 1

39 FRUITS

THERE ARE

12   **8**   **5**

40 MATH

THE ANSWER IS 1

EXPLANATION

equation 1 - (9 - 5) X (9 - 5)
= (4 x 4) = 16 (First subtract
the bigger number by the
smallest then multiply it with
the same number)

equation 2 - (6 - 4) X (6 - 4)
= (2 x 2) = 16

equation 3 - (8 - 3) X (8 - 3)
= (5 x 5) = 25

equation 4 - (2 - 1) X (2 - 1)
= (1 x 1) = 1

42 FARM

There are **2** hens with 3 legs.

43 SPELLING

1. surprise
2. coming
3. again
4. tomorrow
5. February
6. which
7. decided
8. piece
9. once
10. should
11. because
12. forty
13. beautiful
14. through

(1). 35 – 20 – 3 – 7 – 1 = 4

(2). 23 + 5 – (15 + 14 – 4) = 3

(3). (42 ÷ 6 + 9) × 5 – 2 = 78

146

A.2

B.4

C.3

D.1

E.6

F.5

SOLIDS: chair, apple, rock

LIQUID : milk, juice, rain

GAS: perfume

66 COUPLE

67 INSTRUMENTS

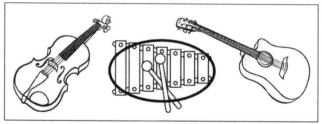

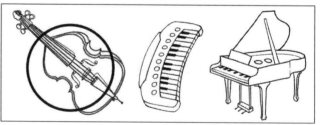

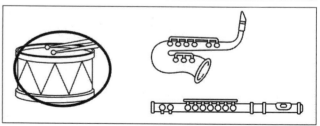

147

1.

2	4	1	3
1	3	4	2
3	1	2	4
4	2	3	1

2.

1	2	4	3
4	3	1	2
2	4	3	1
3	1	2	4

3.

1	4	3	2
2	3	4	1
4	2	1	3
3	1	2	4

4.

3	4	2	1
2	1	3	4
1	2	4	3
4	3	1	2

1	2	4	6	3	5
5	6	3	1	4	2
3	5	1	4	2	6
2	4	6	5	1	3
4	3	5	2	6	1
6	1	2	3	5	4

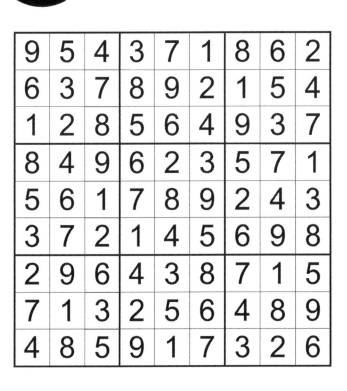

9	5	4	3	7	1	8	6	2
6	3	7	8	9	2	1	5	4
1	2	8	5	6	4	9	3	7
8	4	9	6	2	3	5	7	1
5	6	1	7	8	9	2	4	3
3	7	2	1	4	5	6	9	8
2	9	6	4	3	8	7	1	5
7	1	3	2	5	6	4	8	9
4	8	5	9	1	7	3	2	6

STEPS IN THE CORRECT ORDER

6 → 1 → 2 → 5 → 3 → 4

76 FROG

 77 WATER

1. B   2. A   3. D   4. C

STEPS IN THE CORRECT ORDER

$$\underline{1} \rightarrow \underline{4} \rightarrow \underline{3} \rightarrow \underline{2}$$

	TRUE	FALSE
1.	✓	
2.	✓	
3.		✓

 79 BE PRESENT

 81 SUMMER

THE STORY IN THE CORRECT ORDER

$$(c) \rightarrow (d) \rightarrow (a) \rightarrow b) \rightarrow (e)$$

149

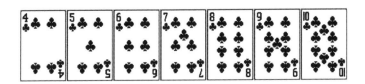

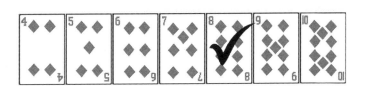

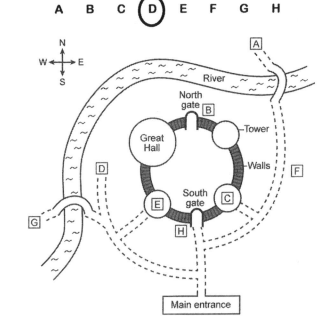

A B C D E F G H

1. PACIFIC OCEAN
2. NORTH AMERICA
3. ATLANTIC OCEAN
4. AFRICA
5. SOUTHERN OCEAN
6. EUROPE
7. ASIA
8. INDIA OCEAN
9. AUSTRALIA
10. ANTARCTICA
11. SOUTH AMERICA

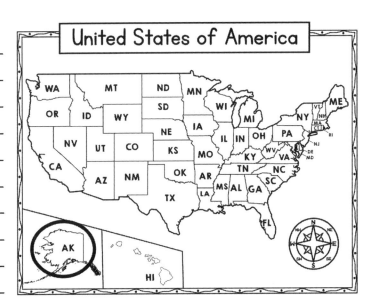

150

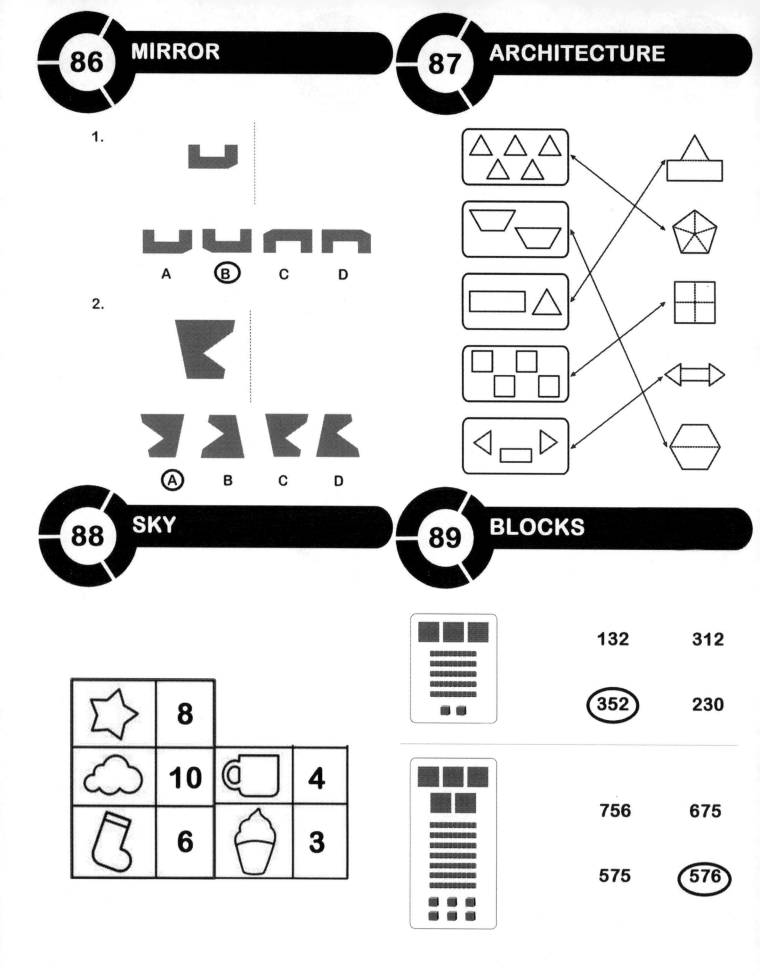

1.

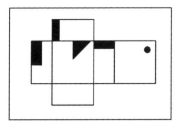 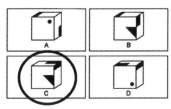

2.

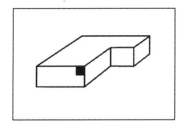 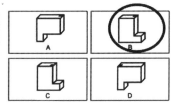

1.C

2.A

3.C

4.A

5.A

(1) 1865

(2) Union

(3) soldiers

(4) slavery

(5) reconstruction

```
H C H I L D R E N X H E F Y S S
C O M F O R T A O Y S R Q N R C
T Y A E L U G C K A M Y A A W O
E C V R Z Q L Z E K T R C T E N
L J Z T U S W R A I E W G G O S
E A K I V F C I R T E C Y I S U
V A H L S N X E E N K M T D P M
I R C I I H P V M Q O A R Y A E
S V I T Y S D Q S N L A P Q P R
I E X Y O Z H E O U C L Q J A I
O G R R K J D C P T T A E S R S
N R P N I I E O I Y I T U Q T M
S D R P J K P D M A Q Z J X M C
D C O U N T E R C U L T U R E C
M R L P V R S U B U R B S K N C
E K A J C P O S T W A R X O T U
```

TRUE   FALSE

1. ☐ ✔
2. ✔ ☐
3. ✔ ☐
4. ☐ ✔
5. ☐ ✔
6. ✔ ☐
7. ✔ ☐

1. 1901
2. 1917
3. 1929
4. 1941
5. 1963
6. 1964
7. 1969
8. 1974

98 WOMEN'S RIGHT

99 AIDS EPIDEMIC

1g

2e

3f

4h

5a

6d

7b

8c

(6) → (1) → (4) → (5)

→ (3) → (2) → (7)

100 NUCLEAR POWER

101 DUCKS

HOW MANY DUCKS ARE THERE?

12

1.

Hiroshima and Nagasaki

2.

Soviet Union

102 DICE

EXPLANATION

Each line has two dice of the same color and numbers: 2,3, and 5. So the answer is

103 MATH

1. The family has six kids – five sons have one common sister.

2. I have so many problems.

3. This aunt is Isabella's mom.

4. Each kid will get four cookies.

5. Since all months are 30-31 days long, and February has either 28 or 29 days, they all have 28 days.

6. No, it won't be sunny weather because it will also be midnight in 48 hours.

104 CAR

The parking spot number is 87.

EXPLANATION

To solve this you'll need to look at the puzzle from a different angle. What you see are inverted numbers, the actual sequence is 87, 88, 89, 90, 91.

105 CODING

The correct answer: 0 4 2

EXPLANATION

Five clues are below:

6 8 2 - One Number is correct and well placed

7 3 8 - Nothing is correct

2 0 6 - Two Numbers are correct but Wrong Places

6 1 4 - One Number is correct but wrong placed

8 7 0 - One Number is correct but wrong placed

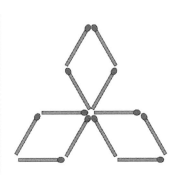

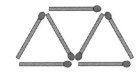

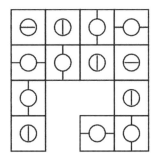

1. There are 40 squares.

EXPLANATION:
Big block 1
Small blocks 16
The center squares 2
Inside the center squares 8
2×2 block squares 9
3×3 block squares 4
No. of squares = 1 + 16 + 2 + 8 + 9 + 4 = 40

2. There are 17 squares.

EXPLANATION:
If you consider the smallest square to be of 1 unit;
Then there are;
6 squares of 1 unit side,
8 squares with side 2 unit,
2 squares with ide 3 unit
and
1 square with side 4 unit.
No. of squares = 6 + 8 + 2 + 1 = 17

108 INTELLIGENCE

1.

2.

    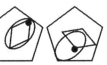 ?

YES ☐

NO ☑

The answer is Thursday.

EXPLANATION:

Note that Thursday, Friday, and Saturday are 3 consecutive days. If she wrote on a Wednesday, and it is given that she wrote on a Thursday, Friday and Saturday. Then it says that she wrote for 4 consecutive days which can't be true. Thus, she did not write her blog on that Wednesday.

EXPLANATION:

The only day they both tell the truth is Sunday; but today can't be Sunday because the lion also tells the truth on Saturday (yesterday). Day by day, the only day one of them is lying and one of them is telling the truth with those two statements is Thursday.

Made in the USA
Columbia, SC
17 November 2024